PENGUIN BOOKS

SECOND WIND

Nathaniel Philbrick is the *New York Times* bestselling author of *Valiant Ambition*, winner of the George Washington Prize; *In the Heart of the Sea*, winner of the National Book Award; *Mayflower*, finalist for the Pulitzer Prize; *Sea of Glory*; *The Last Stand*; *Bunker Hill*; *Why Read Moby-Dick?*, and *Away Off Shore*. He lives on Nantucket Island.

ALSO BY NATHANIEL PHILBRICK

VALIANT AMBITION:
*George Washington, Benedict Arnold,
and the Fate of the American Revolution*

BUNKER HILL:
A City, a Siege, a Revolution

WHY READ *MOBY-DICK*?

THE LAST STAND:
Custer, Sitting Bull, and the Battle of the Little Bighorn

MAYFLOWER:
A Story of Courage, Community, and War

SEA OF GLORY:
*America's Voyage of Discovery;
The U.S. Exploring Expedition, 1838–1842*

IN THE HEART OF THE SEA:
The Tragedy of the Whaleship Essex

ABRAM'S EYES:
The Native American Legacy of Nantucket Island

AWAY OFF SHORE:
Nantucket Island and Its People, 1602–1890

THE PASSIONATE SAILOR
(illustrated by Gary Patterson)

Second Wind

A Sunfish Sailor, an Island,
and the Voyage That Brought
a Family Together

Nathaniel Philbrick

PENGUIN BOOKS

PENGUIN BOOKS

An imprint of Penguin Random House LLC
375 Hudson Street
New York, New York 10014
penguin.com

First published in the United States of America
by Mill Hill Press 1999
Published in Penguin Books 2018

Illustrations by Laura Hartman Maestro

LIBRARY OF CONGRESS CATALOGING-IN-PUBLICATION DATA
Names: Philbrick, Nathaniel, author.
Title: Second wind: a sunfish sailor, an island, and the voyage
that brought a family together / Nathaniel Philbrick.
Description: New York, New York: Penguin Books, an
imprint of Random House LLC, 2018. | First published in the
United States of America by Mill Hill Press 1999.
Identifiers: LCCN 2017024034 (print) | LCCN 2017055169 (ebook) |
ISBN 9780525503835 (ebook) | ISBN 9780143132097
Subjects: LCSH: Philbrick, Nathaniel. |
Sailors—Biography. | Sailboat racing.
Classification: LCC GV810.92.P52 (ebook) | LCC
GV810.92.P52 A3 2018 (print) | DDC 797.1092 [B]—dc23
LC record available at https://lccn.loc.gov/2017024034

Printed in the United States of America
1   3   5   7   9   10   8   6   4   2

Set in Adobe Caslon Pro

DESIGNED BY KATY RIEGEL

To Melissa, Jennie, and Ethan

Contents

Author's Note

I NEVER THOUGHT I would have a midlife crisis. As far as I was concerned, all of life was a crisis. To point to a single event as the defining moment of one's middle age was either a baby boomer's self-dramatization or, at the very least, wishful thinking. Doesn't the word "midlife" imply that you've got more than a few good years left?

I've now come to realize that the events described in this book, all of which occurred between the spring of 1992 and the fall of 1993, constituted, if not a crisis, a kind of watershed. Before that year, I was a stay-at-home dad who only got out of the house to take my two kids to the playground. While I considered myself lucky to be with my children every day, I had lost almost all touch with sailing, the sport that had once meant everything to me.

Then everything changed. For reasons I'm still trying to understand, I decided to take another shot—maybe one last shot—at the Sunfish championship I'd won fifteen years before.

I began an odyssey that led me from the lonely ponds of Nantucket Island to a humbling return to competition in Florida, then down the Connecticut River with my family before I headed out to a steamy lake in Illinois for the North American championship. In the end it brought me home, to Nantucket. That all this happened while I was working on a history of the island called *Away Off Shore*—a book that tells of a place experiencing its own midlife crisis—makes me scratch my ever-lengthening forehead and admit that, well, maybe its author was having one, too.

✿

Now, twenty-five years later, my wife Melissa and I still live on Nantucket. Although I have long since donated my Sunfish to the island's community sailing school and we recently traded our beloved Beetle Cat for a more comfortable Herreshoff 12½, we still sail every chance we get. Our daughter Jennie grew up to be a highly competitive Laser sailor and was a member of a nationally ranked sailing team in college. Our son Ethan, never a serious racer, has become the most adventuresome mariner of us all, whether it's circumnavigating Cape Cod in a small cruising boat or dodging the tugs on the Hudson River in a J/24. Just last summer, I'm happy to report, Melissa and I took our two-year-old granddaughter Lydia on her first sail across Nantucket Harbor.

Many of the books I've written since the publication of *Second Wind* in 1999 are about America's relationship to the sea. This is the book with which I explored my own relationship to both salt and fresh water, and I hope you enjoy the voyage.

—NATHANIEL PHILBRICK
Nantucket, April 2017

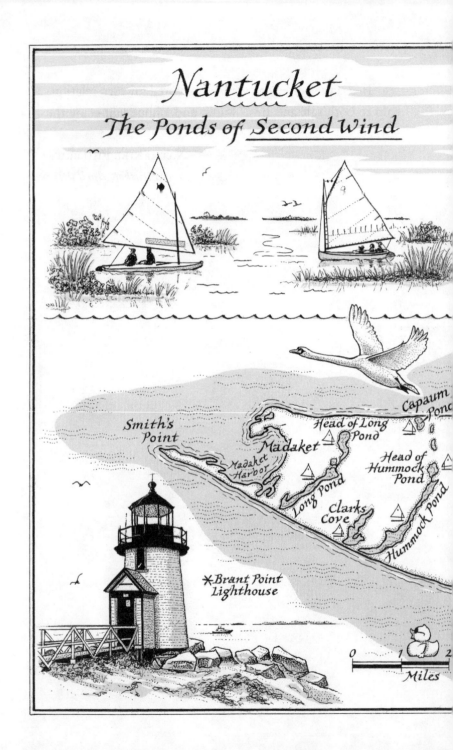

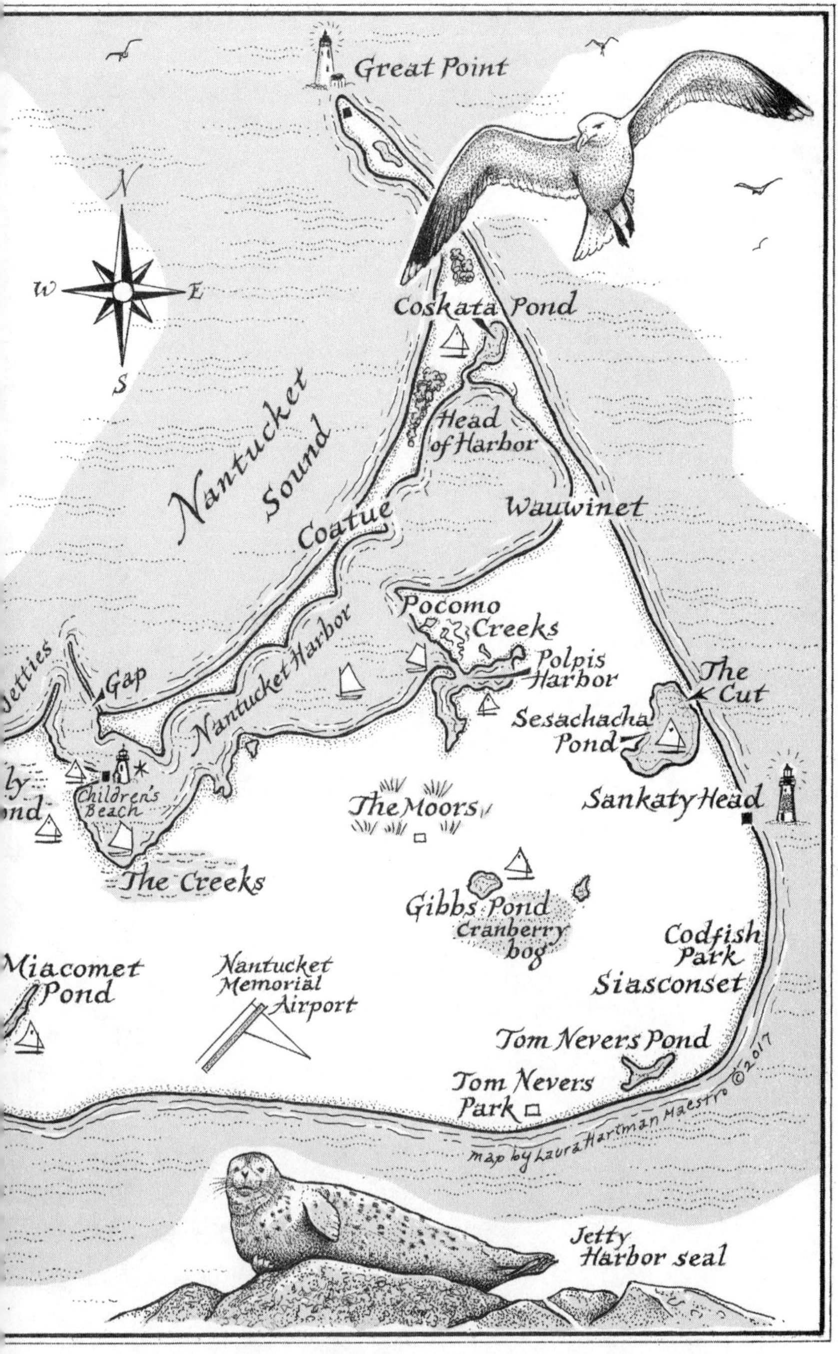

Great Point

Coskata Pond

N
W E
S

Nantucket Sound

Head
of Harbor

Coatue

Wauwinet

Pocomo
Creeks

Polpis
Harbor

Nantucket Harbor

The
Cut

Jetties

Gap

Sesachacha
Pond

Children's
Beach

The Moors

Sankaty Head

...nd

The Creeks

Gibbs Pond
Cranberry
bog

Codfish
Park

Miacomet
Pond

Nantucket
Memorial
Airport

Siasconset

Tom Nevers Pond

Tom Nevers
Park

Map by Laura Hartman Maestro ©2017

Jetty
Harbor seal

Second
Wind

Prologue

MY CHILDREN GLARED AT ME. What they saw was pathetic: their thirty-six-year-old father watching television on a weekday afternoon. It wasn't *Oprah* or *Geraldo* or *Donahue*. It was worse. I was watching the America's Cup on ESPN.

The thing of it was, I hated the America's Cup. Having grown up racing little sailboats on little lakes, I had nothing but contempt for what the announcers kept calling "the holy grail of sailing." To self-styled purists like me, the Cup was more about money and ego than wind and water. If there was an essence of sailboat racing, the America's Cup had moved about as far away from it as San Diego was from Newport.

Then what was I doing in front of the television?

The kids wanted to watch *The Mickey Mouse Club*, but I wasn't about to surrender the remote control. As a parent I could decree it was my turn, not theirs. The race might not even be close, but I was going to see the finish.

It was a contest of wills, and I was going to win.

"Dad," said nine-year-old Jennie, "get a life."

"Yeah," added six-year-old Ethan as the two of them turned and headed out the door. So there.

I tried to concentrate on the television screen, but something nibbled at me, made me shift restlessly on the couch as the two giant yachts glided across the nearly windless Pacific Ocean.

Maybe it was time for some fresh air.

The kids had gone off to play Frisbee in the backyard. They had already forgotten about the scene in the living room, but I hadn't. Although they let me join their game, it wasn't long before my attention drifted toward the side of the house where my old yacht, a dirt-encrusted Sunfish, leaned against the foundation.

If an America's Cup boat is a Ferrari, a Sunfish is a VW Bug. Some would not even call it a sailboat—just a piece of recreational equipment. Real yachtsmen like Sir Thomas Lipton and the Vanderbilts wouldn't have been caught dead in a Sunfish. The boat is so mundanely bourgeois that John Updike used one to kill off his middle-class archetype, Rabbit Angstrom.

But to me a Sunfish was more than a water toy. It might be ugly—an ironing-board hull with an isosceles-triangle sail—but a Sunfish is fast. When I sailed a Sunfish for the first time at the age of fourteen after two years of poking around in an eight-foot pram, I felt like I had traded a paddleboat for a torpedo boat. No wonder Jack Kennedy sailed these boats. There's even a picture of him on a Sailfish, the

Sunfish's even more humble predecessor, sporting the same grin he flashed from the bridge of PT-109.

The notion of racing a Sunfish might have struck even the classy JFK as absurd. It's low to the water, it's wet, it's . . . undignified. But for me in 1970, a teenager in desperate need of an escape from all the land-based problems of the world, there had been something elemental and all-consuming about a Sunfish. Nothing could compare to the exhilaration of a close race in a real blow—the wind howling and spray flying as my Sunfish and I punched through the waves to the finish.

But on that spring afternoon in 1992, Sunfish racing seemed about as irrelevant to my life as the America's Cup. Instead of a sailboat, this sap-spattered fiberglass hull, unused in more than a decade, looked like a beat-up luggage pod waiting to be clamped to the roof of a minivan.

By that point I'd abandoned Frisbee and was standing beside the Sunfish. Eventually the kids wandered over to see what I was up to.

"Give me a hand," I said.

I grabbed the Sunfish's gunwale, Jennie took the stern, and Ethan wrapped his little fingers around the handle at the bow. Together, we lowered the hull onto the grass, right side up. What had been nibbling at me while I watched the America's Cup turned into a stabbing pain in my gut.

Scribbled across the deck in grease pencil were the compass headings from my last big regatta: the 1978 North American championship, the highlight of my sailing life, when at twenty-two years of age I had eked out a narrow victory over 178 of the most competitive Sunfish sailors on the continent. Although I had sailed and even raced the boat a few times since then, I had never let myself erase those hieroglyphics with their mystical significance to my golden age.

A car pulled into the driveway. It was Melissa—my wife, the kids' mother—returning from a day at the office. Jennie and Ethan ran up to greet her, and soon all four of us were staring at the Sunfish.

"What are you going to do with *that*?" she asked.

Melissa had also been a sailor. In fact, we had met as sailing instructors at a yacht club on Cape Cod. From the beginning, however, there had been profound differences in the way we approached the sport.

Although Melissa had been an extremely talented sailboat racer who had finished second in the 1981 Women's Sunfish North Americans, she never seemed to take it terribly seriously. Sailing was just one of the many things she had done well as a teenager growing up on Cape Cod.

For me, on the other hand, sailboat racing had been more like a personality disorder. By some cruel twist of fate, my father's search for tenure as an English professor had marooned our family in Pittsburgh, Pennsylvania, but that only made me more stubbornly committed to becoming a world-class sailor. Whether it was on the Monongahela River or a man-made lake, I spent just about every weekend jousting against my younger brother Sam in a Sunfish.

In high school I was one of three thousand students and painfully shy. In a Sunfish, however, my inhibitions dissolved. With a mainsheet in one hand and a tiller extension in the other, I attacked each race with a passion that only my brother and my parents truly appreciated. During the summer of 1974, my fervor grew to include a girl named Melissa with blond hair, blue eyes, and a sunburned nose. And on a cool, foggy night in August, we ended up together in the cockpit of her family's Beetle Cat, the same kind of 12½-foot sailboat in which both my parents had learned to sail a generation earlier. An eighteen-year-old misfit from Pittsburgh felt as if he'd finally found the place where he belonged.

The following year, Melissa and I, by then a confirmed couple, drove out to a Sunfish dealer in Springfield, Massachusetts. After an unsatisfactory fling with a flashy Olympic-class dinghy, I had decided to return to the boat that had given me my real start. Although Melissa was sometimes bewildered and even frightened by the way I acted around sailboats, she had come to regard my behavior as a kind of insanity that, if not treatable, was at least temporary. That afternoon in Springfield, however, everything was delightfully calm as the two of us wandered hand in hand through a yard full of brand-new Sunfish, in search of the perfect hull.

Seventeen years later, here we were, assembled around that same boat. Needless to say, it no longer looked perfect.

"Why don't you ever sail it?" Jennie asked.

It was a good question.

Not long after Jennie's birth, I had made the decision to pursue a writing career at home. Life became a blur of doctor appointments, diaper changes, deadlines, and rewrites. The prospect of doing anything that did not somehow revolve around writing or around the schedules and needs of Jennie and Ethan became unimaginable. My sailing exploits seemed to have been performed by another person a long time ago. I took it for granted that the self-absorption sailing required of me would have been toxic to the life I now led. I dared not even talk about those days out on the water, as if the mere mention of a sailboat might puncture the cocoon of domesticity I had so carefully spun for myself. Just look at what havoc one televised race had wreaked.

Jennie said it. "You should sail again, Dad."

I turned to Ethan. "What do you think?" I could feel Melissa's eyes studying me.

Ethan shrugged. "Sure," he said.

I began to wonder: Could I climb back into the cockpit of this beat-up old boat and still be the father and husband I had always been? Was this what I needed to "get a life"?

Part I
A Pool in the Stream

Take almost any path you please, and ten to one it carries you down in a dale, and leaves you there by a pool in the stream. There is magic in it. Let the most absent-minded of men be plunged in his deepest reveries—stand the man on his legs, set his feet a going, and he will infallibly lead you to water, if water there be in all that region. Should you ever be athirst in the great American desert, try this experiment, if your caravan happen to be supplied with a metaphysical professor. Yes, as every one knows, meditation and water are wedded for ever.

—HERMAN MELVILLE, *Moby-Dick*

The Race

I SHOULD HAVE KNOWN BETTER. You can't just "get" a life.

Six years earlier Melissa and I had tried to do exactly that by moving to the island of Nantucket, twenty-four miles off the New England coast. We had grown tired of living and working around big cities; we wanted more time with our children and with each other; and besides, back then we had both hoped to sail again. Perhaps on Nantucket, once the mother ship of American whaling, we could create an environment for our children in which we were all, figuratively, if not literally, in the same boat.

But it didn't start out the way we had planned. Melissa soon found that life as an attorney on a real-estate obsessed island was as demanding as it had been in the city. For my part, being a housebound writer and parent on relatively tiny Nantucket was even more claustrophobic than it had been in the suburb we had previously called home. An island is a tough place to be landlocked.

But there was more to it than that. Something dark and disturbing would occasionally punch through the surface, reveal just a hint of its massive, lugubrious bulk, then vanish again, only to reappear at the strangest of times. I began to sense that something weird, huge, and scary was, well, out there. And then one February afternoon I saw it—a whale.

It had been back in the days when Ethan still fit comfortably on my shoulders. We were on one of our daily walks along the south shore of the island when the kids and I found ourselves on a bluff overlooking a winter beach and a crowd of people clustered around the black lifeless shape of a young humpback, less than twenty feet long. In her death spasms she'd vomited her stomach lining, and the placenta-like mess floated in the waves beside her. Two men with clipboards and waders measured the carcass and took notes. Children clambered over the whale's smooth, rubbery body, bouncing on her upturned belly as if she were a trampoline. That February afternoon, with my daughter beside me and my son perched on my shoulders, I first realized that it was time for a change. Like that youthful whale, I was stranded. At some point, I would have to return to the sea.

By the spring of 1992, I was working on a history of Nantucket that gave me a renewed appreciation for the island's maritime traditions. And even before I'd made that America's Cup–induced resolution to get back into serious racing, I found myself making another sailing-related commitment: I had agreed to run the sailing program at the Nantucket Yacht Club. I'd always assumed my days as a sailing instructor were behind me. But Jennie and Ethan were growing up, and as a seasonal position, the job dovetailed nicely with my life as a writer.

That summer Melissa and the kids were given the opportunity to race a borrowed Beetle Cat (known as a Rainbow on Nantucket), the same kind of boat in which Melissa and I had had our first date. Although I was happy for them, it was also frustrating. As they won an impressive number of blue first-place flags, my yacht club duties required that I remain rooted to an NYC support boat. I felt left out of my children's introduction to the sport that had been so important to my own coming of age. And what about me?

As the summer passed, the conversation around the dinner table was becoming unendurable.

Jennie: "How many flags have we won so far?"

Ethan: "Four."

Jennie: "But they're all blue."

Ethan: "I know. I'd like a red one."

Jennie: "Or how about a yellow one?"

Ethan: "Mommy, can we come in third next weekend, please?"

It was clearly time for someone to put my wife and especially my children in their place. By the end of July, I'd come up with Plan Gordon.

Gordon was new to the sport. A marathon runner and bike racer, he had purchased a Beetle Cat only the year before. Although he was obviously in tip-top shape, he lacked the experience to race competitively and was becoming frustrated. He needed some tactical advice and instruction. What he needed, I decided, was me. One Saturday morning

I happened to run into Gordon on the yacht club lawn. It was soon agreed that I would crew for him in the first race after I had assisted my staff in setting up the race course.

Part of the beauty of Plan Gordon was the element of surprise. Melissa and the kids would have no idea what they were up against until the last possible moment. And, as luck would have it, they were over on the other side of the harbor when I jumped from the yacht club's mark boat into Gordon's Beetle Cat.

With only a few minutes before the start, I fiddled with the various adjustments to the sail in an attempt to optimize its shape. As I stared up at the flapping panels of Dacron cloth and tugged on some lines, Gordon questioned me about what I was doing. Although I tried to answer as best I could, I found myself irresistibly looking out for the competition: a white Beetle Cat with a green sail and three members of my family on board.

An air horn sounded, indicating that we had three minutes before the start. With a familiar rush of adrenaline, I reached involuntarily for the tiller, but there was Gordon—and he needed some pointers. I told Gordon to sail over toward the committee boat. That's where Melissa and the kids were hanging out, their sail luffing lazily as Ethan dangled his hand in the blue, sun-glinting water. These guys wouldn't know what hit them.

On my cue Gordon tacked, turning us so that we crossed into the wind and ended up beside Melissa, our sail also luffing. The rest of the fleet of about five other boats was behind us, which was good—as long as we didn't cross the line too early.

"Hey, Daddy!" Jennie shouted. "What are you doing out here?"

I chose to ignore her. I did notice, however, that her mother was looking straight at me. Melissa knew exactly what I was up to.

We were down to the last thirty seconds, the most critical time, with that green-sailed Beetle beside us. Ethan, the collar of his yellow lifejacket pressed up against his chin, looked under the boat's sail.

"Hi, Daddy!" he called out.

Once again, I chose to ignore him.

"Daddy!"

"What?" I finally said.

"How ya doin'?"

"I'm doing—"

The starting horn blew, and in a blink of an eye Melissa and company were off. Okay, so I was a little late pulling in the sail, and maybe that's why they were able to surge ahead of us, but if Ethan had just not distracted me . . .

Since sails flutter uselessly like flags when pointed directly into the wind, a sailboat must approach the first "upwind" mark indirectly, tacking back and forth across the course. And where a Nantucket whaleman thought in terms of weather systems and continental currents as he navigated the oceans of the world, a modern small boat racer approaches each momentary change in the wind as if it were a storm front, each point of land as if it were Cape Horn. This hypersensitivity to the elements means that the first leg of a typical race becomes a panicky, zigzag quest for the fastest path to the windward mark.

And as it so happened, halfway up the first leg we caught a nice wind shift on the right-hand side of the course and were suddenly back in contention. Gordon was doing an excellent job of steering the boat, and yet I found it impossible not to be a micromanager, offering a continual stream of advice: "Toward the sail a little bit . . . now away from the sail . . . that's it!"

The first mark of the race was a torpedo-shaped buoy anchored in the harbor channel, not far from the long barrier beach, known as Coatue, that forms the outer edge of Nantucket Harbor. Since the entire, seven-mile length of the harbor empties and fills around the end of this giant sand spit, the current there is usually quite fierce, as much as three to four knots. But all concern for the current was temporarily suspended when I realized that we were battling for first with Melissa and the kids.

The conservative thing for us to do would have been to duck behind Melissa and then tack, essentially following her to the mark. But I was not about to yield. It was all or nothing. I told Gordon that with one perfectly executed tack we could knife in between Melissa and the mark. He looked underneath the sail to see what lay ahead. What he saw obviously worried him. "Are you sure?" he asked.

But by then it was too late. "Tack!" I shouted. As Gordon jammed the tiller over, I realized that I had made a terrible mistake. The tide was rushing in much faster than I had realized. Try as I might to get us moving forward instead of sideways in the current, we were soon wrapped around the buoy.

There is nothing worse than being pinned against a mark in a strong tide. It's humiliating, particularly when your wife and children sail past singing "Found a Peanut."

There are no referees in sailing; it's up to the competitors to discipline themselves. If you commit a foul, by hitting a mark or another boat or by getting in someone else's way, you can exonerate yourself by sailing one or two complete circles (depending on the seriousness of the transgression) as a penalty. It is not a fun maneuver, and after disentangling ourselves from the mark and doing our penance, I apologized to Gordon. To his credit, he seemed completely unflustered by the incident. Who cared if we were now in third? We were still in the hunt, with plenty of race left to sail.

The wind was now from behind, putting us on a broad reach to the next mark. It turned out that Gordon's boat was fast on this point of sail, and we were able to round the next mark in second. Melissa and the kids were still quite a way out ahead.

Then it happened. Suddenly, and for no apparent reason, that green-sailed Beetle turned around and headed right for us. I could see Jennie up on the bow, her long blond hair flowing back in the breeze as she pointed at something in the water while Ethan shouted excitedly from the cockpit. Then, just before we came abreast of them, Melissa spun the boat around, the sail swooping across dramatically as Jennie plunged her hand into the water. The kids began to cheer. What was going on?

Waving a sodden baseball cap in the air, Jennie explained: "I dropped it overboard and Mommy went back to get it."

Melissa smiled and shrugged. I didn't know what Gordon was thinking, but this was more than I could stand. This was a race. To turn back for a stupid hat was unthinkable, particularly when you were in first place. The implication was clear: I can do almost anything and still win.

The gloves were off.

We rounded the last mark with Melissa less than a boat length ahead of us. With one, relatively short upwind leg before the finish, it was time to make things happen. So we tacked in an attempt to find a shift of wind that would help us. But Melissa wasn't about to let us get away with it, tacking almost immediately to position her sail between ours and the wind. So we tacked again—as did, of course, Melissa. It was, in the parlance of the America's Cup commentators on ESPN, a tacking duel to the death.

Beetle Cats are too heavy to tolerate too much tacking, but we put our boats through their paces. Luckily, the boat in third was unable to take advantage of our infighting, and we were still neck and neck going into the finish. On board our boat, the tension was palpable: my hands trembled with excitement; Gordon's eyes blazed with competitive fire.

It was a replay of the first leg. Melissa was approaching the finish line on one tack; we were on the other. The plan, once again, was to suddenly tack just ahead of her, shoot up into the wind, and grab the victory. If it was close, I figured my boys on the committee boat would give us the nod, knowing that their jobs depended on it. I warned Gordon of the impending maneuver, and both of us were glancing toward that green-sailed menace when Gordon laughed. He laughed!

"Will you look at that!" he cried.

"What?" I shouted. "What?"

"Look at your son!"

I squinted through my salt-spattered sunglasses. Ethan was leaning against the combing of the cockpit, his head wobbling drunkenly with each bob of the boat. My God, the kid was asleep! Asleep? At a time like this? Didn't he know he was in the midst of a tacking duel to the death?!

That, I must admit, took the stuffing right out of us. Slam-dunking a mother and her sleeping babe is a difficult thing to do, even if you are the husband and father. By the time Gordon and I pulled ourselves together, it was too late. The moment to pounce had passed, and when we did eventually tack, Melissa walked right over us and took the gun. The worst part was that she and Jennie didn't cheer; otherwise they might have disturbed Ethan.

Up a Creek

BEFORE I KNEW IT, Labor Day had come and gone and the kids were back in school. Time for me to leave the waterfront behind and become a writer again.

But after two weeks researching old documents, I was thinking about sailing again. The Gordon debacle still stung, but I knew that there had to be more appropriate ways to work out a decade and a half's worth of stifled sailing frustrations than taking on my wife and kids in a Beetle Cat. I knew that relief could only come in a Sunfish.

By the end of September I'd learned that the 1993 Sunfish North Americans were to be sailed on a man-made lake in Springfield, Illinois, in July. Illinois? In July? Wasn't it kind of ridiculous, venturing to the Land of Lincoln from the Island of Ahab?

For me the site had one undeniable advantage, however. Lake Springfield was notorious for its light winds. Since I was no longer in the physical condition I'd been in fifteen years before, the lighter the wind, the better. But there was another consideration. By traveling to Lake Springfield I would be, in a sense, returning home.

We had moved to Pittsburgh when I was in first grade, and one of my earliest and most vivid memories of the place is of a ride our family took up the Monongahela River in a motorboat. Having previously lived in Burlington, Vermont, we were all shocked and horrified by just how industrial the place was: steel mills, barges, tugs, and—everywhere we looked on that hot summer afternoon—catfish floating on the river's surface, either dead or gasping for oxygen. Soon enough, though, we had replaced the motorboat with a small sailing dinghy and moved our boating from the river to a series of man-made lakes.

For the next several years, my brother Sam and I had preferred to stay onshore, either fishing or collecting crayfish while our parents sailed back and forth across the lake, almost always within sight, occasionally waving and calling out to us. At some point Sam and I had asked for a sailing pram of our own, and then, a few years later, a Sunfish, and we raced every weekend on the new and relatively large lake at Moraine State Park, about an hour outside the city.

Although I hadn't been to Pittsburgh in over a decade, I still looked back fondly at that lake, a body of water so placid, so hemmed in by trees and houses that sailing was more like a walk in the park than a journey into the wilderness. At Moraine, I was free to explore every vagary of the wind with a spontaneity and abandon that the ocean, with its tides, waves, and fogs, rarely permitted. Now, after more than seven years on a tiny island at the edge of the sea, I could still feel the pull of a liquid speck in the heartland of America. Springfield would be just fine with me.

But one question remained: How to prepare for a regatta on an inland mill pond when I lived on an offshore island with the highest average winds in New England?

⁂

On a Sunday at the end of September I went for a sail, but not in a Sunfish. I was once again in the Beetle Cat, but this time with Melissa and the kids. This was to be our last sail together before we pulled the boat out for the season, and I wanted to make the most of it. Also at work was an indistinct need to somehow redeem myself after that summer's catastrophe on the race course. My wife and children, however, were in no mood for a sail. According to them it was too cold, 55 degrees and breezy, and the three of them huddled together in the windward corner of the cockpit, complaining every time a droplet of spray flew in their direction.

In the southwestern corner of Nantucket Harbor is an area known as the Creeks. It's the ultimate tidal estuary, a meandering mile through a wide plain of beach grass. Earlier that summer I had explored the Creeks in a small Boston Whaler, and I had inevitably found myself wondering what it would be like to sail down this intimate country lane of an inlet, so unlike the waters surrounding Nantucket.

As long as the tide was flowing out, I knew we couldn't get into too much trouble. If the tide was coming in, however, we'd have our work cut out for us when it came time to escape from this marshy maze. Sailing against both the current and the wind on a river that was only fifteen feet wide would be next to impossible.

So what was the tide doing? I glanced at a nearby dock. The pilings looked to be wet above the waterline, indicating, I assumed, that the tide was indeed going out. All systems were go.

I kept my plan to myself as we sailed past a virtual forest of wintersticks, the white pieces of wood that take the place of mooring balls in the off-season. Up ahead were the sheds and Quonset huts that comprised a shipyard. Beyond it lay the Creeks.

By now we were steaming along with the wind behind us on a run. Without the frequent tacking and spray in the face associated with beating against the wind, a run tends to be a much calmer, more laid-back point of sail. But we were in no position to relax. The shoreline was coming up fast and Melissa and the kids wanted to know what I had in mind. So I told them. They said it was a dumb idea; we didn't have enough time if we were going to pull out the boat that afternoon as we had originally planned. I assured them that it was going to be just a short, casual side trip; that the current would help us zip out of there in no time.

Meanwhile, we were running out of water, and I was having a difficult time finding the mouth of the creek. It blended in with the beach grass and was proving very tough to spot from a distance. The centerboard was already halfway up, and it was scraping on the sand. I ordered Melissa to raise it all the way. Although Melissa and I first met while teaching sailing, the honeymoon was over a long time ago. As she pulled up the centerboard, Melissa began to mutter mutinously.

Just before I thought we were going to end up on the beach, I found the creek entrance. But why was the tide so low? Shouldn't it be higher if my calculations were correct? But there was no time to speculate. Hugging the right bank, we barely made it over a sandbar and then, WHOOOOOSH! we were on our way, running at a good clip down a very narrow and curvy waterway. The creek went right. With the centerboard up, the Beetle skidded around the corner, and we bumped up against the bank, our wake cresting on the shallows behind us. This was beginning to feel like a ride in Disney World. But what about the tide? No doubt about it, the tide was coming in.

I knew we should turn back. But all of us got caught up in the speed of our journey as we whizzed along, our sail bellying out over the marsh grass. A snowy egret looked up, thought about flying away, but stayed and watched us pass, less than three feet away. Beneath us we saw, with an intense and startling clarity, a sunken motorboat. On and on we sailed, following this narrow, curving strand of water until we had been transported into a wide and wonderful no-man's-land of cattails and waving grasses.

As we approached a private dock with several boats tied to it, I realized that there wasn't enough room for us to make it past without crashing into the creek bank. So, after putting the centerboard down as far as it would go, I shoved the tiller over. But instead of cutting across the current, we slid sideways into the muddy bank, pockmarked with fiddler crab holes. Melissa pulled out the paddle and, between pushing and paddling, forced our bow around so that we were pointed into the onrushing current. The breeze filled our sails and off we went, the water gurgling past.

It sure felt like we were moving right along.

"Daddy, look!" Ethan shouted.

Over on the creek bank there was a fiddler crab. He was scuttling over the mud, and he was passing us. We were going nowhere against the stream at three knots. Then the wind died and we slid backward into the bank. No amount of paddling was going to get us out. Given the current, there was only one alternative: Daddy had to get dirty.

Taking a line with me, I leapt onto the bank. The mud seemed firm, and I began to pull. They were a canal boat, and I was the mule.

After a few minutes of trudging over the marsh mud, as my wife and children heckled me unmercifully, I hit quicksand. Actually, it was more like quickmud. First I sank up to my ankles, then my knees. Soon I was waist-deep in marsh muck—the rank, sulfurous scent of decay sweeping over me in eye-watering waves. Needless to say, the crowd on board the Beetle went wild.

But I was too distracted to notice. Through a break in the marsh grass I could see the distant saltwater pond that marked the end of the Creeks. Compared to the burbling, mud-fringed frenzy of this tidal stream, that distant pond exuded a sun-dappled sense of absolute serenity. It looked very much like the nearly windless puddles that Mom and Dad had so cheerfully sailed, beckoning my brother and me to join them. Then it hit me.

I would sail the Nantucket equivalent of the man-made, midwestern lakes of my boyhood. I would sail the ponds. There are close to twenty of them on the island; some of them are relatively large, some are microscopic, but almost all would be sailable in a Sunfish. Part Joshua Slocum, part Thoreau, I would voyage from pond to pond until I arrived at my final destination—the Sunfish North Americans.

In a Bog

It was Columbus Day weekend. Five hundred years since that legendary sailor had first laid eyes on an island in the Caribbean, my own island was to be the site of a more personal voyage of exploration. There was one hitch, however. Over the summer the English ivy that flourishes around the foundation of our 150-year-old house had wormed its roots into the aluminum lip of my Sunfish's gunwale. When it came time to put the boat onto the car roof, I literally had to tear it away from the house. Hunks of dirt were caked along the lower edge of the boat. Dispossessed potato bugs ran screaming for cover. In the Sunfish's cockpit a reddish-brown soup of rainwater, leaves, and what looked like the ancient remains of some kind of food proved that life may have indeed evolved from the ooze. Wedged between the boat and the ivy-covered house was my badly mildewed spar bag. I didn't even want to think about what the sail inside looked like. Melissa and Jennie were scheduled to be "off island" (a Nantucketer's version of "out of town") that weekend with another mother and daughter doing some heavy female bonding in Boston. That left Ethan and me on our own, and Ethan was about three feet too short when it came to helping me get the 135-pound Sunfish on and off the car roof.

Then my old college roommate Marc called up to ask if he and his new girlfriend could come to the island for a quick visit. Now I had all the brawn I needed, and on Sunday morning, with the grimy Sunfish strapped to the roof and with Ethan, Marc, his girlfriend Beth, and our dog Molly all crammed into our Colt Vista, I set out in search of my first pond to conquer.

Since downtown Nantucket and the waterfront were still crowded with tourists, I thought it best to make a tactical retreat to the Moors, one of the island's more inaccessible areas. This gently rolling landscape is graphic evidence of Nantucket's glacial origins. Known technically as a knob and kettle landform, the Moors originally came into being when large chunks of ice became mixed up with the sand and gravel deposited by the melting glacier more than fifteen thousand years ago. When the buried ice chunks melted, deep hollows (or kettles) were formed, creating a wavelike terrain dotted with small ponds.

A hundred years ago, sheep kept almost the entire island closely cropped. Since then much of Nantucket has become overgrown with either trees or houses, but these Moors, officially known as a heathland, have remained, for the most part, much as they once were. A network of dirt roads crisscrosses its undulations. As you drive up and down the hills, it's easy to lose your bearings, and it wasn't long before I hadn't a clue where we were.

Marc, who has never been one to keep his thoughts to himself, wondered how there could possibly be a pond in a place that looked so much like the surface of the moon. Ethan complained that all the up-and-down motion was making him carsick. Way in the backseat, jammed among my rudder, lifejacket, and other sailing paraphernalia, Molly the dog was clearly not happy.

It was Beth who spotted it first.

"Look! Water!"

There was Gibbs Pond, a quarter-mile circle of blue. Just beyond it was the deep red of the Windswept Cranberry Bog, the largest natural bog in the world. Harvesting had just begun.

In the seventies Gibbs Pond had been the site of an annual Thanksgiving Sunfish regatta. With the class in its heyday, up to twenty island boats would attend. Now I was the sole keeper of the faith. In any event, it was as good a place as any to begin my training program.

Unfortunately, there wasn't much wind. An almost preternatural stillness reigned, marred only by the distant drone of the cranberry pickers' machinery. Marc helped me lift the boat off the roof and carry it down a narrow path to the water's edge. Beth and Ethan threw sticks for Molly as I scrubbed the deck. With a final pause, I sponged away the grease pencil marks, the last clues, perhaps, to an earlier self.

But if the hull was now a blank slate, the sail was another matter. All those years in the spar bag had created a giant Rorschach test of mildew, a bloated amoeba of filth that seemed about to ingest the much smaller Sunfish insignia. My racing steed was an embarrassing mess.

I pushed off for a solo spin around the pond, but I was finding it next to impossible to concentrate on sailing. For one thing, there was barely enough wind to fill my sail. For another, there was all this natural beauty. Within the hollow of these autumn-tinged hills I was inching across a trembling mirror of blue, brown, red, yellow, and green. I was also floating on the lid of a time capsule—a receptacle filled with ancient glacial runoff and the accumulated stones, bones, and artifacts of ten thousand years of human habitation.

In what I remembered as my prime, I had sometimes found myself in a kind of mental tunnel, a narrow corridor of absolute concentration that I used to call the Zone. All sports have it—a point at which what once seemed so difficult and complex becomes, at least for a time, astonishingly simple, a matter of instinct. Along with this Zen-like sense of certainty, the Zone has a more ruthless side, a very un-Zen-like competitiveness—a need to win. Did I care enough anymore to fight my way back into the Zone?

I thought of Ferdinand, a character from a children's story I had read repeatedly to Jennie and Ethan. Ferdinand isn't like other young bulls; instead of wanting to fight and strut his stuff at the bullfights in Madrid, he wants to remain in his pasture, sitting quietly in the shade of a cork tree and smelling flowers. Now I wondered whether I could both sniff the flowers and rouse myself to gore the matador. Given that there wasn't any wind, sniffing the flowers looked like my only option.

I beached the boat and invited Ethan, Marc, Beth, and even Molly to come aboard. Skeptically, they all squeezed under the low-slung, race-rigged boom, and we headed to the far side of the pond to watch the cranberry harvesters. It's hard to fit that many people and a dog on a Sunfish. I stood on the stern holding the tiller. Ethan stood on the bow and held on to the spars while Marc and Beth sat with their feet in the cockpit. Molly cowered near the splash rail, desperate to have it over with.

We landed beside an old pump house used to adjust the water level of the bogs. For most of the year the bogs are relatively dry, but during harvest season they are flooded and threshed with a machine that looks like a combine on stilts, and the berries all float to the surface. Just as we arrived, the workers were collecting the berries into a huge blanket of brilliant red that they then fed to a conveyor belt that carried the berries to an awaiting dump truck.

As we sailed back, fog began to appear along the edges of the pond. By the time we were once again in the car, the road was showing dimly through the mist.

The wipers slapped across the windshield, and I strained to see what loomed ahead. Marc asked, "You going to do this all winter?"

"That's the plan," I said.

"What exactly is the plan?"

"A pond a week. I figure there's at least a winter's worth of them, all different shapes and sizes."

"You'll be sailing even in February?"

"That's the plan."

We drove on in silence. After a while, he said, "Think you'll win it again?"

"Well, it doesn't look so good right now."

Marc turned and looked out his side window into the fog. "No, it doesn't."

If today's sail hadn't moved me much closer to becoming a competitive Sunfish racer, I still had faith. And the only way to proceed was one pond at a time.

The Green Gush

At dinnertime on Friday of the next week, the phone rang. It was a long-distance call for Melissa. Being a small-town lawyer, she gets more than her share of business calls at dinnertime. But Nantucket isn't an ordinary small town. Now that the island has made the transition from a world-renowned whaling port to an equally famous summer resort, it is still globally connected.

A client was calling from Hong Kong, where the sun was rising to a new morning. On Nantucket he owns a large house situated on a narrow bluff between Sesachacha (pronounced SACK ah cha), one of the bigger ponds on the island, and the Atlantic Ocean. In recent years the pond, and Melissa's client, had been in the midst of a controversy. For hundreds of years the town had been "opening" the pond to the sea on a biannual basis, a flushing process inherited from the Indians. Besides allowing for the migration of herring, the opening also helped control the growth of algae and weeds in the pond. Then, about a decade ago, the state environmental people stepped in and called a halt to this ancient practice. Soon the pond became choked with weeds; billions of midges began to buzz over the water; the pond started to die.

Finally, after a local vigilante went to jail for digging a trench with a shovel and opening the pond himself, the state relented and allowed the town to resume its old ways. Melissa's client owned the land where the trench was traditionally dug and had inevitably become involved in the controversy. Now that everything was legal, he only wanted to be sure that the beach was put back together after the pond had been opened.

Melissa's client had just received a fax informing him that the town planned to open the pond (with as little fanfare as possible) the next morning. A strong southwesterly breeze was forecast, the direction needed to help blow the water out of the pond and keep the trench open as long as possible before ocean currents eventually closed it. Could Melissa please contact the selectmen and make sure all was being done according to the standing agreement?

My training program suddenly gained a new dynamic. I would sail Sesachacha. I remembered hearing stories about the shovel-wielding vigilante getting blown out to sea by the sudden rush of water he unleashed. Through a massive gash in the sand I would boldly sail where no man had sailed before. The next day there was a near gale blowing from the southwest, a weirdly balmy breeze for mid-October. Autumn leaves clattered across the street all morning, but it wasn't until 1:30 in the afternoon that I was able to head out for the pond.

Melissa did not want me to go. She saw the cut across the beach as a kind of bathtub drain, an inexorable suck to oblivion. I preferred to view it in more positive terms: a birthlike gush into the blue salt sea.

Also, Melissa wasn't thrilled about following me all the way out to the east end of the island, helping me off-load the boat, then returning a couple of hours later to put it back on the car roof. Indeed, the prospect of doing this every weekend for the next nine months was not making her very happy. But at least Nantucket was an island less than fourteen miles long, and Sesachacha was about as far away from our house as it was possible to get.

After loading the boat onto the ten-year-old Chevrolet Citation that served as our second car, Melissa followed me in the Vista. The Citation was the quintessential "island car," a vehicle that you wouldn't dare drive anywhere but on Nantucket. The kids called it "the Stinker" because it was the car in which we took the garbage to the town dump. About three months earlier the car had lost second and fourth gear, and not wanting to put any more money into it than I had to, I'd been getting along fine with just two forward gears. Sure, it rumbled a little bit in the transition from first to third, and you couldn't go much more than forty miles an hour, but when did you ever need to go any faster on Nantucket?

I half expected to find the pond sucked almost dry, but all seemed relatively normal as Melissa and I lugged the boat down to the water's edge. The kids were at the high school pool watching a swim meet, so it was just the two of us. On the opposite side of the pond we could see a backhoe surrounded by about half a dozen pickup trucks. A cut had obviously been made in the pond side of the beach, and yet there was no swirling rush of water cresting around the opening. All looked static, even serene.

Melissa waited until I had pulled up the sail. Even though we were sheltered by a clump of trees, the sail flapped like a flag in a hurricane; it was really blowing.

"This is crazy," Melissa said.

"I know," I said, zipping up my lifejacket.

"It's dangerous."

"This is a pond. Even if my mast breaks, I can walk back to the car."

"But what about the opening?"

"I'll keep clear of it, I promise."

"Remember," Melissa said as she turned to go, "you have two children." A particularly strong puff came through. Melissa said something else, but I couldn't hear her over the flogging sail.

With the rudder down and the daggerboard halfway in, I jumped onto the boat, gave the sail a few tugs with the mainsheet, and was off on a run. The boat immediately leapt onto a blinding plane, the kind of plane in which the boat wobbles side to side like an X-15 rocket plane about to burst through the sound barrier. If I remembered correctly, it really had to be blowing for a Sunfish to behave like this on a run. And the farther I got from the windward shore, the more the wind increased. By the time I was in the middle of the pond, I was holding on for dear life. And up ahead, spread wide like the gaping jaws of a huge beast, was the cut.

Before I got any closer to the cut, I decided that I better round up and test the breeze more carefully. As soon as I did, I was socked with what must have been a thirty-five-knot puff. As I bore back down, the boat took off onto a full-tilt plane, spray flying in all directions. Soon I was zooming past the cut. There was no evidence of any current running out into the ocean.

Then with a puff of smoke from its exhaust pipe, the backhoe began to lumber toward the ocean side of the beach. So that was it—the opening had not yet been completed. This was something I had to see. I decided to park the boat near the cut and watch the show.

The breeze was so strong that a mountain of frothy pond scum had accumulated on the shore. I hauled the Sunfish through the brown foam onto the beach. It was a long trudge through the ankle-deep sand to where they were digging. The people assembled there (a few civic types and some fishermen) looked at me as if I had just arrived from the planet Mars, and that's exactly how I felt, standing there in my soaking wet sailing coveralls and lifejacket.

"Nat!"

I turned and saw Laura, a friend and member of the Conservation Commission. She had a surfcasting rod in her hand. "I had no idea it was you until I read your name on the back of your lifejacket."

Laura explained that they'd been waiting for the tide to go out all the way so as to maximize the difference between pond and sea levels. Now it was dead low and time to finish the cut. As the backhoe moved up and down the trench, widening and deepening it, the water gradually increased to the point that it finally burst through in a green rush that quickly carved out a twenty-foot-wide opening. Minnows leaped in the flow as some of the fishermen began casting out into the ocean in the hope that these minnows would act as bait for bluefish and sea bass. The backhoe driver gunned his engine and roared away just in time to avoid having his rear wheels undermined by the flowing water.

It soon became obvious that, even if I had wanted to, there was no way I was ever going to sail through the cut. It was too narrow and its banks were too steep to accommodate a Sunfish with its boom all the way out. Perhaps it was just as well.

Saying good-bye to Laura, I headed toward my boat. The hull was now almost completely buried beneath the scum. Clearing it away as best I could with my hands (it felt like a mixture of Cool Whip and marsh mud), I pulled the boat out into the water. I now had two hours of heavy-air sailing ahead of me within the confines of a small but big enough pond. It was just the kind of practice session I was looking for.

When the wind is strong, the sail generates more lift than the boat knows what to do with, causing the boat to tip, or heel. To keep the boat from capsizing, a sailor "hikes out" by leaning out as far as possible on the side opposite the sail and using his or her body weight to keep the boat from heeling. If the force of the wind is so strong that the boat continues to heel even though the sailor is hiked out all the way, it's time to reduce the pressure on the sail by letting a portion of it flap, or luff. This is accomplished in one of two ways—easing the mainsheet or using the rudder to turn the boat in the direction of the wind. When it's blowing hard, a sailor spends most of the race hiked out while constantly adjusting the mainsheet and rudder to keep just the right amount of drive in the sail. It can be exhausting work, particularly over the course of an entire day of racing.

Whether or not the people on the beach had anything to do with it, I don't know, but I began my upwind beat like a hotdogging kid, grimacing heroically as I pumped the sail and rocked my upper body in the puffs. Two minutes into this shameless display of muscles I didn't have, however, my body caught up with me. Soon I was hunched over on the deck, trying to catch my breath, and I wasn't even a quarter of the way up the pond.

Rather than telling the boat what to do, I began to figure out what the boat wanted me to do. A black cat's-paw of wind tore up the pond ahead, and instead of letting the boat stagger in the puff, I eased the mainsheet, hiked a little harder, and then gradually trimmed the sail. The simple discipline of analyzing my movements distracted me from the pain my body was experiencing. It was as if I had stopped flailing my way across a swimming pool and stumbled across the basic mechanics of the crawl.

Two hours later, I was standing on the launch ramp beside my Sunfish. I was totally exhausted, and yet I felt oddly energized. At one point during my sail—I wasn't sure exactly when and for how long—I'd approached a Zone-like state, a flickering sense of focused intensity during which nothing except the boat, the wind, and the water had seemed to matter. If it wasn't exactly like riding a bicycle, at least it was still possible for me to reestablish some semblance of how it used to feel in a sailboat.

Soon Melissa and the kids drove up, honking the horn and waving. A sandpiper that had been patrolling the beach beside me took to its wings as Jennie and Ethan ran down the ramp, chattering about the swim meet. Melissa followed soon after.

"How'd it go?" she asked.

"It's a start," I said.

As the two of us lugged the boat back to the car, I realized that like this newly opened pond, something inside of me had begun to break free.

Love's Handiwork

I KNEW THERE WAS at least one pond on Nantucket I would never sail. Lily Pond is the name given to a low, marshy section of bottomland in the northwest corner of Nantucket town. In the early 1700s it had been a true body of water about the size of Gibbs Pond. Lily Pond was extensive enough and deep enough that the townspeople had built a fort on an island in the middle in case of Indian attack. At an earthen dam in the easterly corner of the pond, where a restaurant now stands, was a fulling mill for processing wool, and fishermen wintered their sailing vessels in the lee of the dam. For a small island community in which sheep raising was still as important as whaling, Lily Pond was the town's focal point.

Then something happened.

One afternoon in the early 1700s a twelve-year-old girl named Love Paddock was walking home from a friend's house along the Lily Pond dam. She noticed that the waters of the pond were unusually high. Taking up a clam shell, she dug a small trench across the dam, and she watched as water began to trickle through it. Suddenly realizing that she was late for supper, she dropped the shell and ran for home, a house overlooking the pond.

The next morning the girl was awakened by the cries of her father as he gazed out their front doorway.

"O, what a wicked piece of work here is," he shouted.

"What is it?" asked his wife.

"Some evil-minded person has let the Lily Pond out. It has run away the sand and made a great gully. The fulling mill is gone, and the fences torn up. Several small vessels have received damage, and some boats stove to pieces. A great deal of damage is done."

The girl trembled in her bed in terror. What should she do?

On her deathbed sixty-eight years later, Love Paddock asked that her neighbors be sent for. Once they were gathered, she told the story of what had really happened to Lily Pond. Not until the 1840s was her confession made public.

If I couldn't sail Lily Pond, I could at least walk it. But I needed a guide: Wes Tiffney, director of the University of Massachusetts–Boston Nantucket Field Station. Wes is a great bear of a man, with stiff dark hair and, if it's sunny, Wayfarer sunglasses. A plant biologist who has developed into the island's premier erosion specialist, Wes was just the person to fill me in on the science of ponds.

It was a dazzling blue Indian summer afternoon, and as we drove around what Wes said had once been the perimeter of the pond, the slanting yellow light seemed to evoke a sense of ancient, yet redeemable time. The outline of the old pond was clearly discernible as a rough triangle made by three streets. It was amazing. For more than seven years I had been completely oblivious to this dried-up pond bed, the evidence of which now screamed at me. It was not unlike oceanographers finally uncovering the evidence of the meteor that may have killed off the dinosaurs. The remnants of the pond had been there all along, right underneath our noses.

Most of the old pond bed is now conservation land. Wes and I parked and followed a vague trail across a well-kept meadow punctuated by trees and wetlands. Every now and then Wes would stop to look at his compass and check the topographical map. He also took time to point out any interesting plants, always providing me with their Latin names. As we made our way across this craterlike depression, Wes filled me in on the nature of ponds.

As landmasses go, Nantucket is about as close to being a sponge as you can find. Since the island is mostly sand, rain, and snowmelt percolate right through it until they reach a level at which all the spaces between the sand and gravel particles are already filled with water. Since fresh water is less dense than salt water and the two don't mix very well, a lens-shaped mass of fresh groundwater actually floats on a layer of salt water that extends beneath the island and, for that matter, all of Cape Cod. Eventually, the fresh water moves downward and seaward, finally overflowing the edges of the island or escaping through springs in the shallow ocean bottom.

Why hadn't Lily Pond filled right back up again after Love pulled the plug? Perhaps the town fathers decided to leave well enough alone and not rebuild the dam. Surviving town records suggest that the demolished mill had never been very successful. As Wes pointed out, given the lay of the land, the pond could never have generated very much power for a mill. Maybe the area was more useful as fresh and extremely fertile farmland than it had been as a mosquito breeding pond.

Wes also reminded me that the first English settlement on the island was not where the town stands today. Instead it had been situated to the west where a small circular harbor once existed on the north shore, a harbor that has been known for 250 years as Capaum (pronounced Ka PAWM) Pond. In the early 1700s a violent gale threw up a sandbar across this little harbor, sealing it off from Nantucket Sound. With what had already become a too-small anchorage on its way to becoming a freshwater pond, the Nantucketers decided to move their settlement east to its present location. It had been about this time that little Love Paddock took up her clamshell. With land values beginning to rise in the vicinity of the new harbor, no one was in a hurry to reclaim Lily Pond.

That weekend I would voyage not only in space but also in time. I would sail from the new to the old harbor.

Time Travel

It was a Saturday, the day after Halloween, and a whole new order of weather had set in—gray, cold, and winterlike. I wasn't equipped for temperatures this low. My two-piece dinghy suit and fingerless sailing gloves were designed for summer. What I needed, what I planned to buy, was a dry suit, a one-piece suit with rubber gaskets at the neck, wrists, and ankles to keep the water out. But for the time being my old equipment would have to do.

By now I was deep into my research on the history of the island, and I emerged from my basement study around noon, feeling strangely animated, juiced on the idea of validating the mental probings of the last few months by doing something in the real world. During lunch with Melissa and the kids, an on-island friend named Mark called, asking if I'd help him put his rowing dinghy on his car roof. He was taking it in for the season. I agreed, on the condition that he'd help me heft the Sunfish. We scheduled to meet at a beach by Nantucket Harbor.

Although this meant that Melissa didn't have to help me unload the boat, she wasn't happy with the situation. Sailing around like a maniac in a pond was one thing, but venturing out of Nantucket Harbor, then sailing for a couple of miles all by myself in open water before I landed on what might be a dangerously wave-washed beach and then dragging my Sunfish across the sand and through the cattails into a pond, well, this was conduct hardly becoming a reasonable person. It was dangerous, foolhardy, dumb. Did I know how cold it was out there? How windy?

I admitted that I hadn't left the house yet. I pointed out that since the wind was coming from the north I'd be blown back toward the island instead of out to sea if anything did go wrong. Before leaving, I promised that if it looked too bad, I'd return after helping Mark.

Of course I had no intention of returning. In fact, by the time I made it down to the harbor, I emerged from the Stinker like a man possessed, slapping my hands together and squinting into the wind (my God, it was blowing hard!) and shaking Mark's hand.

Mark designs houses. He is precise and careful, even meticulous. He had spent the last two years restoring a lovely twenty-three-foot pocket cruiser in his spare time—refiguring the interior, refinishing the teak deck, etc.—and whenever he ran into a job that required another pair of hands, I'd help out. Mark's attention to detail, his devotion to doing it right, was truly inspiring.

By comparison, I was a slapdash slob. After my windy sail on Sesachacha, large numbers of the sail sets—plastic curtain-hanger rings—used to attach the sail to the spars were either undone or missing altogether. I rummaged through the fetid back of the Stinker for line and improvised as best I could. Finally, I began to put on my dinghy suit. Mark had been extremely restrained as he watched me making it up as I went along, but now he was really worried.

"Nat, don't you have anything warmer?" he asked.

I explained that I was planning on purchasing a dry suit.

"But you're going to freeze."

"I'll be okay."

With my Pittsburgh Pirates baseball cap firmly lodged on my head, I pushed off into the harbor. Since this section of the anchorage is basically a tidal flat, I had to beat away from the shore with my daggerboard halfway up—not an easy maneuver, especially since the boom had to be manually lifted over the top of the raised daggerboard with each tack. Finally I made it into deep water, and with a final thank-you wave to Mark, I was on my way.

Now that I was on the water, the realities of my situation began to catch up with me. What a cold, bleak day. The sky was low and gray, an overhang of slate above the harbor. It seemed more like evening than early afternoon. I felt an almost erotic stirring of fear. This was dangerous. My equipment was, to say the least, iffy. A rudder could break; my halyard was frayed; I could capsize, lose the boat, and die of hypothermia.

At least I had a few compatriots out here on the water. A couple of fishermen were testing their boats in preparation for the first official day of scallop season. The average Nantucket scallop boat is the nautical equivalent of an island car: a floating junk heap that limps along for three months until the scallops run out and is then dumped back in the yard for another nine months of quiet deterioration.

Today I felt a certain kinship with the scallopers. My boat was still a mess. Sap-sealed dirt glazed the hull, giving it the appearance of a speckled egg. My daggerboard was so nicked and gouged it looked as though I had used it to beat back a shark attack. And, of course, there was my mildewed sail. The scallopers and I might not be maintaining our boats in "Bristol fashion," but, hey, who had the time for it? Our boats got the job done. At least I hoped my Sunfish would get the job done.

The wind was coming directly out of the harbor entrance, making it a dead beat to windward. By the time I had reached the Coast Guard station at Brant Point, just across the channel from the tip of Coatue, my hands were numb and white. But I didn't stop to warm them up. I was in too much of a hurry.

Given the inadequacies of my clothing, it was in my best interest to complete the passage from here to Capaum Pond in as little time as possible. Melissa and the kids were scheduled to meet me in less than two hours, and I knew they'd worry if I wasn't there before they arrived. Being in a rush also made it feel more like a race, and for the time being this was as close as I was going to get to simulating regatta conditions.

So I continued past the Brant Point lighthouse, blowing on my hands and wiggling my fingers as best I could. The entrance to Nantucket Harbor consists of two long break-waters that extend out from Jetties Beach to the west and Coatue to the east. This creates a rock-rimmed corridor that accelerates the current and increases the size of the waves, especially when the wind is against the tide—exactly the conditions I had today: a twenty-knot northerly with an ebbing, south-flowing tide.

Just as I rounded the lighthouse I began to hear a distant, menacing roar. I knew almost immediately it must be the sound of the waves breaking on the jetties, but it wasn't until I saw the leaping foam on either side of the channel that I began to appreciate what I was in for. Wow. This made Sesachacha look like the kiddie pool.

Well, at least the feeling was coming back into my hands. As I approached the Coatue shore on port tack, the wind shifted to the right, heading me dramatically. So I tacked and followed the lift along Coatue, where seagulls and cormorants roosted by the hundreds on the sand. As I sailed past, only a few yards away, the birds took flight, squawking and flapping their wings and momentarily distracting me from what lay ahead.

Then I saw the waves: so big and gray that each white-capped crest seemed capable of crushing my little boat beneath an icy avalanche of water. These were the kinds of waves that belonged in the open ocean. In a minute I would be among them in an ever-narrowing passageway bounded by jagged rocks.

What if I turned back? Could I return to the house before Melissa and the kids set out to retrieve me? If I missed them, they might panic. If they showed up at Capaum Pond and I was nowhere in sight, they'd immediately think the worst. I glanced at my watch and did a few mental calculations. Meanwhile my noble Sunfish continued to blast along against the tide and the wind. I glanced nervously through the plastic window in my sail and scanned the shoreline to the west, where the shuttered windows of some of the biggest houses on Nantucket offered little comfort.

It was then, as I mulled over the possibility of a tactical retreat, that a slanting shaft of miraculous sunlight pierced the clouds. With the sun blazing at an angle from the forbidding sky, it looked like a Thomas Cole painting. Then another shaft of sun punched through, this time up ahead and to the north: a spotlight trained on a distant bell buoy, now Technicolor red in a Caribbean blue sea. Then yet another shaft of light appeared, this one trained on *me*, its pure light bleaching out the Sunfish's sail until it glowed like the cottony clouds they're supposed to have in heaven. Was it a sign?

I was on starboard tack, about halfway into the gauntlet, waves bursting against the jetties on either side of me as the seas inside the channel continued to increase. Instead of the short steep chop I'd experienced the weekend before, which had knocked against the Sunfish's hull like body blows, these waves were so big that I was riding up and then down them, a rolling carnival ride that required me to head up the face of the wave before bearing off down its back.

I knew there was a white buoy at the end of the west jetty, but all the turbulence at the harbor mouth was making it hard to find. There it was—streaked with rust and bobbing crazily in the waves. Once I reached that marker, I could begin to turn away from the direction of the wind and follow the north shore of the island toward Capaum Pond.

As soon as I eased the sail and bore off around the buoy, my Sunfish leapt onto a plane. Sheets of spray funneled into my face, smearing my glasses with salt. Up ahead, about three miles away, I could make out a black water tower and radio transmitter in the general vicinity of Capaum Pond. But I needed more to go on. I knew there was a large white house on the shore beside the pond, but it was difficult to distinguish against the beach. Then another one of those shafts of sun broke through, and, yes, there was that great big gorgeous house lit up like a beacon. Now I could start to enjoy the ride.

Given the course I was sailing, I found it fastest to hold on to each wave for as long as possible, planing across the wave face like a surfer at Waikiki. It was wild, exhilarating, and terrifying, knowing that the forces I was flirting with could easily tear me from my Sunfish and leave me to wash up on the beach like that dead whale.

Before I knew it, I was coming up on the shoreline. As any sailor will tell you, a lee shore is dangerous, and this shore was about as lee as it got. In a Sunfish, the trick is to spin the boat around before a wave has the chance to capsize you against the shore. I was searching for a good place to land when I noticed a purple Isuzu Trooper parked beside a dune. It was Mark. He jumped out and started to point to the west, indicating that I should land closer to the big white house. I planed up to the beach, pulled out my daggerboard, spun the boat around into the wind, leapt out into the water, grabbed the transom, and hauled the boat up onto the beach.

Mark was holding three things: a camera, a towel, and a bottle of Mount Gay. I was elated and thankful enough to give him a hug, but given that I was soaking wet, I went for the rum instead. Mark explained that after dropping off his dinghy, he'd driven over to Jetties Beach to watch me sail out of the harbor. (Given what he'd seen as I rigged my boat, he definitely had reasons for concern.) He said that once I rounded the Jetty it took me all of fifteen minutes to reach Capaum. Now he offered to help me carry the boat into the pond. We found a trail through a fairly flat section of sand and cattails, and in no time I was sailing again.

My hands still trembling with excitement, I was in no shape to make anything more than a ceremonial circuit of Capaum. In the main body of the pond a flock of swans took off the moment I started sailing in their direction, their wings making a bony, whistling snap. I had never realized how deep the pond was, particularly near the shoreline. No wonder the first settlers had used it as an anchorage, especially since a steep hillside to the west, now dotted with houses, provided protection from the northwesterly gales of winter.

In five minutes I'd completed my sail around the pond. It took some searching, but Mark discovered a trail that led from the water's edge to the access road where his Trooper was parked. It was a tight fit, carrying the hull on its side through this curving, thorny passage, but we finally made it. Since I was more than an hour ahead of schedule, Melissa and the kids were nowhere in sight. So Mark kindly agreed to take me and my boat home.

I couldn't believe it. The voyage I'd thought would take most of the afternoon had been completed in less than an hour and a half, taking me from the mammoth waves at the harbor mouth to the sheltered quiet of Capaum. I also knew that it wouldn't have been half as much fun without Mark. Not only would it have been next to impossible for me to single-handedly haul my boat across the sand to the pond, but I would have been without a witness, an audience. Just as a falling tree doesn't make a sound unless someone is there to hear it, so would I have had a hard time convincing myself, let alone anyone else, that I had actually sailed from Nantucket Harbor to Capaum in a howling November northerly.

As we drove back to the house I made two resolutions: to purchase a dry suit and never again to venture out of the harbor. At least I bought the dry suit.

The Suit

I<small>T WAS MADE OF THICK</small>, blue-and-white Gore-Tex and had black, industrial-strength rubber gaskets at the neck, wrists, and ankles. There was a huge, wax-coated zipper in the back, with a leather strap hanging off it so that I could zip and unzip it myself.

The following Sunday the weather was terrible—33 degrees, nearly windless, and on the verge of rain—and I dressed myself in the new suit with a certain grimness. It was like the ritual scene in a Schwarzenegger movie when Arnold suits up for the final confrontation with evil. But instead of strapping on a bulletproof vest and loading up my rocket launcher, I zipped myself into my new dry suit. Trapped air gave me a hulking, pneumatic look, as if I were ready for a moonwalk or a deep-sea dive. By placing a finger in the neck gasket I could deflate myself, at least partially.

Along with the dry suit, I'd ordered a new pair of sailing boots and a lifejacket. Compared to my old one, the new jacket looked like the kind of thing Schwarzenegger himself might wear. It was tight and rode up high on the chest, making me look impossibly well muscled. Top it off with my sunglasses and my Pittsburgh Pirates hat, and I looked like one mean hombre.

I strutted proudly into the living room, where Melissa, Jennie, and Ethan were sitting on the couch reading a book.

"Hey, guys, whaddaya think?"

"My, oh, my," Melissa said.

"Daddy," Jennie giggled, "expecting a flood?"

"Very funny. Let's get going."

"You're gonna drive like that?" asked Ethan.

"Sure. Want to come with me in the Stinker?"

"No way. I'm going with Mommy."

It was a little weird driving around the island with my lifejacket on, and shifting gears in my sailing boots was a challenge. But as I drove the Stinker down Pleasant Street with my wife and kids behind me in the Colt, I felt prepared for anything. Let them laugh, I thought.

I might look like the monster child of the Pillsbury Doughboy and the Michelin Man, but on that bleak November day I was my own kind of superhero. I was Pondman.

Steering Without
a Rudder

I T WASN'T LONG before the wind and current were carrying me deeper and deeper into the intricacies of yet another tidal marsh: Pocomo (pronounced POCK ah ma) Creek, nearly identical to the Creeks in which I had wallowed with the Beetle Cat. This, however, was what on Nantucket was known as a "Polpisy" creek. Instead of the commercial buildings that lined the Creeks off the harbor, only a few palatial summer homes dotted the Pocomo shore. The term "Polpisy" refers to Polpis, one of the prettiest sections of the island, centered on a kidney-shaped inlet off Nantucket Harbor, about four miles east of town. In the eighteenth century Polpis was home to a popular tavern where whalemen and their families could have a drink, "throw the bar" (a game rather like horseshoes), and escape the stern Quaker formality of downtown Nantucket.

Even today, Polpis retains much of its out-of-the-way charm. The little dirt road that leads to the public landing is like no other on Nantucket. The densely packed trees on either side of a meandering road make you feel as if you're leaving behind one island—the wild remote place of barrier beaches and treeless moors—and burrowing into another: an intimate world of coves and inlets, where naked sand has given way to marsh grass and where mallards and geese have replaced the gulls. Long after all other pleasure craft have been pulled out of Nantucket Harbor, the eastern end of Polpis serves as a refuge for a motley mix of sail- and motorboats. It was just the place for a light-air, mid-November sail.

My original plan had been to explore the nooks and crannies of Polpis, then leave the boat at the launch ramp for a voyage out into the eastern extreme of Nantucket Harbor on the following weekend. But once I'd followed the narrow and curving Polpis Harbor channel to the verge of Nantucket Harbor, I'd seen Pocomo Creek. Spread out to the east of Polpis, it seemed to be challenging me to give it another try as a creek sailor.

So I dragged my Sunfish across a narrow sand spit and began my voyage into Pocomo Creek. It was just about then that it began to rain. Not a drizzle but a downpour that rinsed away the already light wind. The tide was coming in, whizzing me along on a rain-dimpled conveyor belt of leaden water. I had hoped to follow the creek all the way to its source, but it soon became apparent that if I was to have any hope of getting out before nightfall, I'd better turn back.

In the narrow Creeks up harbor, the pudgy Beetle Cat had been unable to make headway against the tide, but this tidal marsh was more forgiving. The relative agility of the Sunfish was also a help, allowing me to tack back and forth on this slightly wider creek. Even though the current was humming, I was making some progress.

If the weather hadn't been so miserable, this might have been almost enjoyable as I honed the mechanics of my up-wind technique. The secret to success in light air is using as little rudder as possible to steer the boat. Once the rudder strays from the boat's centerline, it becomes an underwater brake that slows the boat like the extended flaps on a landing airplane.

To avoid using the rudder, fast light-air sailors depend on the boat's angle of heel. It works like this: heel the boat to leeward (in the direction of the sail) and the boat turns into the wind (or heads up); heel the boat to windward (what some might call the wrong way) and the boat turns away from the wind (or bears off). The sail can also be used to help steer: to head up, pull in the mainsheet; to bear off, let the sail out.

All of this means that getting the most out of a Sunfish in light air can be a complex and subtle business, in which the skipper is constantly adjusting the mainsheet and the position of his body in an attempt to let the boat steer itself.

Nowhere is the use of the body and sail more important than in the roll tack, the nautical equivalent of a swimmer's kick turn. Instead of simply using the rudder to turn the boat through the wind and onto another tack, the sailor's body weight "rolls" the boat onto the new tack. When done correctly in light air, the sail never luffs, popping from one side to the other with a satisfying snap.

A roll tack requires a great deal of practice before it becomes second nature. But that afternoon I was not just rusty, I was also suffering from the cold. My Pondman suit was not the cure-all I had assumed it would be. My body was hermetically sealed, but my extremities were frozen. What might have been a rewarding training drill was becoming a demoralizing battle against the elements and myself. As the heat drained from my body through my head, hands, and feet, I realized how easy it would be to fall into the annihilating embrace of hypothermia.

By the time I made it back to the launch ramp, the wind had shifted from the northeast to the southwest, and it was snowing. There were near whiteout conditions as I pulled the hull up onto the beach grass, flipped it over, and tied it to a nearby tree. By the time I had slid into the front seat of the Stinker and fired up the engine, feeling was just beginning to return to my hands. My feet, however, felt like chunks of stone as I shifted into first gear, icy water sloshing inside my boots.

Driving back through the snow shower, my feet aching as the blood finally began to flow again, I had a Proustian moment. Suddenly it was twenty years ago and I was driving a VW Bus with my younger brother Sam in the passenger seat, our dog in the back, and a trailer with two Sunfish behind us. Sam and I had spent all day chasing each other over a flooded strip mine in the worst weather imaginable, training for the races of summer. Our faces and hands glowed red as we consumed vast quantities of potato chips and cookies, Elton John's "Goodbye Yellow Brick Road" blasting on the radio. Between the elevated highway and the

Monongahela River, the stacks of a steel mill pumped pollution into the air.

It had never occurred to me then how isolated Sam and I had been in our devotion to becoming sailors in Pittsburgh. Now, on a November Sunday on Nantucket, I missed my brother and those cold weekend afternoons, towing our sailboats back into the vast, smog-shrouded city.

Death Roll: Coskata

THAT WEEK MY grandmother died. My daughter's namesake, Jennie Kramer Dennis, had lived into her nineties in a retirement home on Cape Cod. Toward the end she passed from a period of terrified paranoia into a warm-and-fuzzy state of befuddlement. Whether this was the natural progression of her senility or the product of nursing-home sedatives, she went out of this life with a whimper, and will be remembered by her great-grandchildren as a pinched, pale face above a long bed with straps across it. The funeral was scheduled for the Monday before Thanksgiving, and, unsure as to whether we were going to be leaving that night or the next morning, I climbed into the Stinker for a Sunday sail in a southwesterly breeze.

Although the temperature was warmer than the weekend before, the sky was just as gray. I found the boat where I had left it, but since the tide was almost dead low, there was a gap of close to twenty yards between the boat and the water. Fortunately, the peatlike muck of Polpis Harbor proved to be as slippery as a damp carpet, and without much trouble I skidded the boat down to the water's edge. As I rigged the sail, I noticed that quite a few scallop boats had relocated to Polpis during the week. One scalloper arrived soon after I got there, not to fish but to work on his boat. In the back of his pickup he had a little dinghy equipped with a single oar off the transom, and in no time he was sculling out across the harbor, working the oar back and forth from a standing position as his forebears had been doing in this harbor for three centuries.

My plan was to sail out of Polpis and head toward the northeast corner of Nantucket Harbor where Coskata (kos KAY ta), a saltwater pond, fed into the harbor through a long and shallow creek. Then I'd venture back west to Pocomo Point, just east of the creek, where Melissa and the kids had agreed to meet me.

Soon I was in the easternmost and broadest lobe of Nantucket Harbor, known as Head of Harbor. With only a low, narrow sliver of sand dividing it from the ocean beyond, Head of Harbor feels like a lagoon at the edge of the universe. But all psychic spaces aside, I was having a more immediate problem of not capsizing in the surprisingly steep chop. With the wind directly behind and the sail out all the way, a charging Sunfish can be a handful. I could see the gusts coming from behind: the water would get dark and rippled and then BAM, the sail would shudder and the boat would roll from side to side, barely under control.

Twice that afternoon I almost capsized to windward, a calamity known as a death roll. The sail went up in the air, I went in the water, and I thought for sure I was about to test the limits of my dry suit as the tips of my hiking boots clung like claws to the forward lip of the cockpit. But each time I was able to save myself with one desperate tug on the mainsheet. Only later did I realize that I wasn't just struggling with the conditions; I was seesawing through the wild mood swings of grief.

Soon Coskata appeared to the northeast, a distant cluster of trees at the convergence of Coatue and Great Point. If it hadn't been for this oasis of oaks and junipers amid a veritable desert of sand, Nantucketers might not have survived the darkest days of the American Revolution. In the winter of 1780, temperatures dropped so low that the harbor froze over completely. All around the island, ice was visible as far as the eye could see. Cut off from mainland supply ships, Nantucketers gradually began to starve and freeze to death. The only remaining source of wood on the island was here, in Coskata, a once-remote area now made accessible because of the harbor ice. Every morning, Nantucketers would set out across the ice, leading their horses and carts through the bitter cold for more than nine miles to Coskata, where they would cut wood and then trudge back across the ice, often returning to town after dark.

Now, more than two hundred years after what became known as the "Hard Winter," Coskata was still home to a dense stand of wind-stunted oaks. The trees grew on a bluff overlooking the stream that fed into the pond, and as I approached on a run, the boat yawing in the puffs and the water getting shallower and shallower, I felt as if I'd already traveled farther than I'd gone in my search for Capaum.

The scrubby bluff loomed like an abandoned battlement. Waves broke on the bar at the creek mouth. Making it across this submerged speed bump was going to be difficult. Even though I knew it would only make the boat tippier, I pulled the daggerboard up so high that not even its tip was poking out from the bottom of the trunk. There was less than four inches of water beneath me.

Running with the wind at a very fast clip atop a mere film of water was a strange sensation. And, of course, there was the now recurrent question: How the hell was I going to get out of here?

Soon the creek began to deepen, enabling me to reach back and push the rudder into a full-down position, and then there was Coskata Pond, a puddle on the eastern edge of America. Beyond this circle of water and a thin margin of sand was the Atlantic Ocean, and three thousand miles beyond that, Portugal.

After a quick, clockwise sail around the pond, I was on my way back. Initially it was kind of fun tacking back and forth up the creek with the daggerboard partway up. But it wasn't long before I had to jump out, lower the sail, and start towing the boat up the creek through knee-deep water. It was an exhausting march back to Head of Harbor, particularly since the wind was howling in my face, but unlike the creeping cold of the previous weekend, I was actually sweating inside my dry suit by the time I made it to the creek mouth.

Soon I was sailing again. Ten minutes into this long, punishing sail to windward I was finding it very difficult to concentrate. As I hung out over the Sunfish's side and mechanically steered through the waves, I kept thinking about my grandmother and grandfather's house on Cape Cod, a shingled mansion inherited from my great-grandfather, a Chicago tycoon. Beside a white sandy beach and a breakwater, there had been an old Sailfish, a rowboat, and a motorboat. For me, this harborside house with its sea breezes and sailboats had been the Garden of Eden, the inspiration behind an adolescence devoted to sailboats. And now here I was, twenty years after the house had been sold, mourning my grandmother's death.

Suddenly a silver pickup truck appeared on Coatue, hurtling west along the beach at an unbelievably high speed. As it fishtailed its way through flock after flock of flapping seagulls, its tire tracks looking like wobbly contrails in the sand, I remembered Grandfather on the lawn, teeing up an old golf ball and thwacking it out into the harbor. But it wasn't just Grandfather whom I remembered that afternoon. No, there, too, was Grandmother in a nearby lawn chair, shaking the ice cubes at the bottom of her glass in a gesture of applause.

Night had fallen when Melissa, Jennie, Ethan, and I boarded the five o'clock ferry for Hyannis. We walked up the two flights of stairs to the main seating area, where we silently shared a pizza. On a Sunday night in November, the boat was almost empty. Against the outer darkness the windows were mirrors, and except for the side-to-side rocking motion, we might as well have been in a train or bus as we began the two-and-a-half-hour ride across Nantucket Sound.

Melissa worked on a quilt, and the kids and I went forward to watch the six o'clock news on the television.

They had just discovered a capsized sailboat off the coast of Ireland—*Coyote II*, a transatlantic singlehander. There was no sign of the skipper, Mike Plant, from Newport, Rhode Island, and only a faint hope that he had escaped to a life raft. My God, I thought, what was three hours in a Sunfish on Nantucket compared to a terrifying capsize and swift, cold death in the middle of the North Atlantic in November?

I was beginning to see that there were limits to my winter sailing. For one thing, the ever-worsening weather made it increasingly difficult to maintain any semblance of concentration beyond an hour or so of sailing. But it wasn't just the cold; there was a corrosive sense of desolation, a blankness out there at the edges of this offshore island that no dry suit could overcome. If I was going to continue, I needed a short-term goal. The North Americans in July was just too far away to give me the required sense of urgency to make it into January.

Sailing's traditional antidote to these doldrums is an institution known as the "Midwinters," a regatta that gives a sailor an excuse to head south and get a sunburn. The Sunfish Midwinters competition was scheduled for early March in Sarasota, Florida. Perhaps I could fly down and charter a boat. It would be expensive, but it might be money well spent. It would be the perfect early warning device, providing a necessary (and potentially devastating) dose of competition with plenty of time left to recover my confidence before the North Americans in July.

Best of all, it would introduce me to the latest crop of

hotshots in the class. As it stood now, the North Americans event was nothing more than a date on my calendar. Beyond some vague, romanticized memories from fifteen years ago, I had no concept of what I was in for, especially when it came to the competition. After an afternoon alone on the rim of the Atlantic, I needed something more than a goal or an event; I needed to draw a bead on some names and faces.

In the Cocktail Glass

By THE NEXT WEEKEND the Stinker had developed a hole in the radiator. The hole was so big that the usual quick fixes were of no help whatsoever. Since I was not about to pay for a new radiator for a car that was already down to two forward gears, I decided to leave well enough alone. Who needed a radiator on Nantucket anyway? The most I ever had to drive at any one time was five or six miles. Sure, the temperature gauge would go sky high, acrid smoke would begin to billow from below the hood, but not once that winter did the engine seize up on me.

The ponds were on the edge of freezing, and on Friday night the temperature dived into the low twenties and the wind died to nothing—the perfect conditions for a freeze. The smart thing to do would have been to go on a reconnaissance mission the next morning, but I was in no mood for being careful. I'd reached a difficult stage in my writing; things were not going in the direction I had planned, and a new direction had not yet made itself clear to me. I wanted to go sailing, and nothing, not even a little ice, was going to get in my way.

I decided to sail Miacomet, a long, narrow, almost river-like pond only a couple of miles from our house. I was still testing the limits of the newly radiatorless Stinker, and besides, Jennie and Ethan were not about to follow Daddy to another pond. By going to Miacomet, Melissa could leave them plugged into the television and get back before any problems developed.

By the time we made it to Miacomet—Melissa behind me in the Colt, the Stinker's yellow warning light blinking in panic—I'd forgotten about the danger of freezing. And sure enough, except for a narrow strip of open water near the far shore, Miacomet Pond was completely covered with ice.

"Well, shall we go back?" Melissa asked.

"What the hell, maybe I can be an icebreaker."

"But—" She stopped herself. Saying nothing, she began to help me unload the boat. She had obviously decided that it wasn't worth debating the point. Still, I detected a certain sense of irritation in the way she drove off down the dirt road, sand spurting from beneath the Colt's tires.

The ice was about a quarter of an inch thick. Once I'd rigged the boat, I used the bow to break an initial gap in the ice, then sheeted in the sail. In the relatively light air the big question was whether I'd have enough power to push my way through the ice.

In a feeble puff, I took off on a beam reach down the pond, busting my way through the ice. It sounded like a toboggan on an icy run—a clattering rattle as the boat was occasionally shunted to the right or left by the ice. At first I feared for my Sunfish's hull, but a quick inspection revealed no damage to the fiberglass. In my wake, bobbing ice chunks formed the precise outline of where I'd been.

Eventually I decided it was time to try sailing upwind, so I jibed around and headed up, with the boat really bouncing around as it carved a turn through the ice. Unfortunately, the wind began to die just as I attempted my first tack. The boat rounded up into the wind but didn't have enough momentum to make it through, and soon I was stuck, at least fifty feet from shore. I started rocking the boat. The squared edges of the hull chomped at the ice, gradually breaking open a section large enough for me to scull over onto the new tack. The sail filled, and I was off again in a rattling rush. Given my frame of mind, it was profoundly satisfying to be breaking up all this ice. I felt like a drunken cowboy busting up chairs in a saloon.

I embarked on a relatively rigorous program of ice-breaking, cutting back and forth across the pond in an attempt to clear out a space in which I could do some normal sailing. About twenty minutes later I had done just that, although the constant tinkling sound of bobbing ice reminded me once again of the ice cubes in my grandmother's cocktail glass, an incongruous summertime sound on an otherwise silent afternoon in winter.

When Melissa finally showed up, she had the kids with her. All Jennie and Ethan wanted to talk about was their movie. At least Melissa was duly appreciative of what I'd accomplished. In what was otherwise a totally frozen pond, there was now a gap the size of a football field. After we'd loaded up the hull onto the Stinker and the kids were back in the Colt and listening to the radio, I jokingly complained to Melissa about the lack of attention my pond sailing was receiving from Jennie and Ethan. They were the ones who had told me, after all, to "get a life."

"Believe me," Melissa sighed, "this is a winter none of us will ever forget."

Strolling Through History

I<small>T WAS THE FIRST WEEKEND</small> in December, known as Christmas Stroll Weekend on Nantucket, when hundreds of fur-coated shoppers from places like Connecticut and New York City descend upon the island for two days of buying and being seen. Downtown Nantucket does its best to look like a Hollywood makeover of itself. Decorated Christmas trees line the sidewalks, shop windows are endlessly teased and fussed with, colored lights and sprigs of holly are tacked to every available surface, and Main Street is closed to traffic. If the Chamber of Commerce gets lucky, a light snow gives the scene a final, perfect holiday touch.

Since prices start to fall in the weeks after Christmas Stroll, locals leave the shopping to the visitors. There is still plenty left to do, however, including holiday caroling, puppet shows, and house tours. But the main event if you have small children is Santa Claus at the Pacific National Bank.

After waiting for an hour in the cold and swirling wind at the head of Main Street, Melissa, Jennie, Ethan, and I finally emerged into the bank's main lobby, a high-ceilinged room with a mural depicting a whaling captain, a whaling merchant, and his bonneted wife, all portrayed as solid, substantial, and quietly heroic.

As we waited in the overheated room for our children to make their supplications to Santa, I couldn't help but feel that the Nantucket I was learning about had little to do with the Nantucket this mural told us there had once been. Indeed, by that point in my research I had begun to feel like a deer attempting to cross an interstate at night, astonished and overwhelmed by flash after flash of, if not insight, at least hints of a Nantucket that seemed utterly strange and new to me, particularly given the island's reputation as an enclave of Quaker righteousness.

There was, for example, the French privateer captain who claimed in 1695 that the island's Indians actually encouraged his crew to pillage the English. According to the Frenchman, the English settlers had turned the Indians into "peasants" and refused to give them firearms. In 1822 a young greenhand from New York wrote in his journal that when his Nantucket whaleship sailed into Hawaii, nearly every sailor "took a wife" for the price of a checked shirt or an old handkerchief. Nantucket whalemen began to sound less like noble pioneers and seafarers and more like the arrogant sailors I'd known in my youth. Was I just playing out the historian's destiny, another generation seeing the past in its own image? I wondered whether in forty years my own account would seem as dated as the bank's mural.

Soon we were standing on the wide stone steps of the

bank. The downward, cobbled slope of Main Street looked like a giant streambed run dry. Jennie, who had merely tolerated Santa, and Ethan, who had pleaded earnestly for a new bike, were each sucking on a lollipop supplied by one of Santa's elves. Melissa squeezed my hand and, assuming we were about to continue our stroll down Main Street, asked, "So what's next?"

I turned from the festive scene before us. "Head of Hummock Pond."

The Jibing Hamster

HEAD OF HUMMOCK was about as small a pond as I could sail on. Even smaller and more perfectly rounded than Gibbs Pond, its surrounding shoreline was also steeper, with high hills that would make an absolute mess of the wind. Since I had sailed Gibbs Pond in a calm, I wanted to try this little kettle hole in a hurricane, and more than thirty knots of wind from the northwest were forecast for Sunday. And besides, Head of Hummock was on the way to the farm where we planned to buy our Christmas tree. Melissa and the kids would follow me to the gravel launch ramp, help me with the boat, then stop by on their way back after buying the tree.

A combination of wind and rain had rid the ponds of ice the week before, but by Sunday the temperature was once again below freezing. When we pulled up to the edge of the pond at about 11:30 Sunday morning, it was barely 25 degrees beneath a thin, blue sky. And the wind had come on as advertised. Dark jagged cat's-paws clawed the surface of the pond with each thirty-knot gust. Random explosions of wind bounced off the hills and caromed across the water.

Beside the launch ramp was a canoe with an icicle hanging off its bow. When Melissa and I took the Sunfish off the roof, a chunk of ice fell out of the cockpit. I knew I wasn't going to last long in these conditions, so I encouraged Melissa and the kids to pick out a tree and return as quickly as possible.

The wind was coming right at the launch ramp, challenging me to launch the boat without getting my feet completely soaked. I pushed the boat into position so that the bow was touching the water and pointed directly into the wind. Then, after adjusting my knitted wool watch cap, I picked up the transom, put the rudder halfway down, took a deep breath, and began to run. Pushing the boat ahead of me like a wheelbarrow, I ran until my feet hit the water, then, with a final shove, I leapt onto the deck, scrambled up into the cockpit, and slipped the daggerboard into the trunk.

I hauled in the mainsheet, the sail filled, and the boat began to move ahead. Now I had to get the rudder all the way down. I was still aft, fiddling with the rudder and congratulating myself on a successful takeoff, when a huge puff slammed into the boat.

I had never capsized that fast before. Usually there is some time to prepare yourself, but this puff was like getting hit by an express train. I had taken such care not to get wet, and now here I was getting thrown headfirst into what might as well have been a vat of acid. But the flesh did not start falling off my bones. Certainly my hands and feet were tingly, but the rest of me was just fine as I paddled around the boat, reached up for the daggerboard, and pulled with everything I had. In a few seconds the boat was back up, the sail was shedding water in the clear cold wind, and I was in the cockpit, desperately yanking in the sail and pumping on the tiller to keep the boat from backing up into the shore. Then the sail filled and I was off.

This was going to be, if not the wildest, most definitely the weirdest sail of them all. The wind was insanity itself, going from five to thirty-five knots and shifting 30 degrees in direction in a matter of seconds. One moment I'd be hiked out all the way, the front half of the sail luffing to prevent me from capsizing to leeward, then WHAM, the wind would shift and die, virtually tacking the sail. Then I'd be on the leeward side of the boat, scrambling to avoid capsizing to windward. Then WHAM, the wind would sock in again from the old direction. I'd tack back, hike out, and wait for the wind to reinvent itself once again. There was no way to anticipate what was going to happen next. All I could do was react as quickly as possible and hope for the best.

As the wind slammed me back and forth, I decided that I had better apply some method to the madness. So I began to sail around the perimeter of the pond in a counterclockwise direction, trying to translate the naked cold force of unharnessed wind and frigid water into the nautical equivalent of a hamster wheel.

By my second lap, I was beginning to establish a routine. I'd sail past the launch ramp on a beam reach and on port tack. Then I'd round up, sheet in, and start to beat to windward along the northern shore of the pond, taking three, sometimes four, very quick tacks. Once up in the northwest corner of the pond, I'd crack off onto a wild reach on starboard, follow the curving contour of the pond until it came time to jibe. This usually occurred where the pond feeds into the much larger Hummock Pond to the south, an area of cattails that I used as an organic buoy—reach the cattails and jibe.

A jibe is the inverse of a tack. You're sailing downwind with the sail all the way out, and you turn the boat away from the direction of the wind till the wind is now coming from the other side. This brings the sail across the boat with the full power of the wind behind it, providing ample opportunity for a capsize if anything should go wrong. And so the cattails became a recurrent crisis point, the place where, ready or not, I had to jibe in thirty knots of wind before I began yet another circuit of the pond.

Head of Hummock is on the edge of a vast tract of conservation land known as Sanford Farm. A trail leads to a hill on the southwestern edge of the pond, and sure enough, two people appeared and stopped to watch me perform my gyrations. What an incongruous sight—a Sunfish planing around a teeny-weeny pond in December! They watched one revolution and were gone.

I was rapidly becoming exhausted, bouncing back and forth across the deck and constantly working the mainsheet and tiller to keep up with the changing wind. By my tenth circle, I found myself glancing over to the launch ramp, looking for Melissa and the kids. The last run from the northwest corner down to the cattails had given me some of the wildest rides I'd ever experienced, especially in the bizarre context of a pond that couldn't have been more than an eighth of a mile wide. But as it turned out, I saved the best for last.

I'd just sailed past the launch ramp when I heard that distinctive honk. There they were, with a Christmas tree on the roof, at the edge of the ramp and waving. I waved back, tacked, and began the sweep along the western edge of the pond. It was then that the biggest puff of the day hit. What began as a fast close reach quickly evolved into a broad reach like none other I had ever known. I was hiked out as far as I could hike; the sail was out and the boat was blasting across the pond, throwing up a blizzard of spray on either side. If only Melissa had had a radar gun. It may have lasted for just a second or two but it was the fastest I had ever gone in a Sunfish. And best of all, it happened in front of my wife and kids.

Call me a showboat, but I launched into that final jibe with a will. I bore off and yanked the mainsheet and jumped over to the new windward side, then headed for the ramp with my afterburners on. After pulling out the daggerboard, I sailed up onto the gravel, my bow coming so close to the car's front bumper that Melissa had to back up to avoid a collision. When I climbed off the Sunfish, the back of my lifejacket was a shelf of icicles. The deck was glazed with ice. Everyone, even Jennie and Ethan, was suitably impressed.

This time Ethan volunteered to drive back with me to the house. Over the blast of the heater we talked about their tree-shopping. Then we talked a little bit about my sail. Ethan had been watching from the backseat, leaning forward between Melissa and Jennie in the front.

"Jennie said you were showing off, but I said you were just sailing."

"You were both right," I said.

Coastal Retreat

ON SATURDAY, DECEMBER 12, Nantucket was hit with what is known as the Hundred Year Storm, the second such storm in two years. Seventy-mile-an-hour northeasterly winds and incredibly high tides transformed the streets of downtown Nantucket into raging rivers. In Siasconset, on the island's east end, seven houses were washed out to sea. All week the local television station repeated a videotape taken of a house, curtains still in its windows and its chimney still intact, getting swept out whole like Dorothy's home in *The Wizard of Oz*. Thirty or more seconds after floating free, the house was savagely ripped apart by the breakers.

For Wes, the scientist with whom I'd walked the grassy crater of Lily Pond, it was like being a kid in a candy store. In the windy, sunny aftermath of the storm, he led a group of erosion experts from the U.S. Geological Survey in Woods Hole around the island. Later that week I talked with him on the phone about the long-term effects of this kind of erosion.

"So how long is the island going to last?" I asked.

"I give it six hundred, maybe six hundred and fifty years."

"What?" Common wisdom on the island put it at two thousand. Six hundred?

"This is how I figure it." In the background I could hear him punching the keys of a calculator. "Right now the island is losing an average of fifteen feet a year. In the next hundred years, global warming is going to double the rate of sea level rise. Since rising sea level is the driving force behind coastal retreat, that puts the annual figure up to thirty feet. Divide that by the average width of the island—about eighteen thousand feet—and I get six hundred years."

I remembered a recent town meeting during which the funding for an environmental study for a "beach replenishment" project, designed to save the homes of several summer residents in Siasconset, was being discussed. One man voiced his opinion that anyone who built on a Nantucket beach was a "damned idiot." But it was a neighbor of mine who carried the day.

"I don't know about you," he said, "but I don't want my coffin floatin' away toward Woods Hole. I say we help pay for that beach."

The warrant article passed.

But were we just kidding ourselves? If this island was indeed doomed to become just another shoal—all its pristine ponds bubbling their groundwater into the salt sea, all our coffins bobbing like Queequeg's in the waves—hadn't we better get used to the idea of the ocean's inexorable rise? Only later, once the rising waters had followed me and my Sunfish into the middle of America, would I begin to appreciate the impossibility of such a reconciliation. To die was one thing, but to be washed away?

Dancing with Seals

By the following Saturday almost all traces of the previous week's flooding were gone from the town waterfront. A mild southwesterly breeze and blue skies made it the perfect day for a December sail. It also made it a perfect day to go seal watching.

Every fall, harbor seals from the north come to Nantucket for the winter. Sometimes you can see them lying on the beaches in the sun, but their favorite hangout is the jetties at the harbor mouth. I'd seen the seals plenty of times from the deck of the ferry. Now I wanted to find out just how close I could get in my Sunfish. Besides, after the defeat of Pondman in Polpis and my funerary voyage to Coskata, I didn't need any more lonely sails. But would the seals be willing to socialize?

It began, at least, in a crowd. Down at Children's Beach, where the launch ramp is one of the few places that offers public access to the waterfront, scallopers who had taken their boats out for the storm were putting them back in.

Melissa helped me unload the boat, then agreed to meet me back at the beach in exactly an hour. No more long, unending adventures in solitude for yours truly. From here on in, each sail would be short and sweet.

Indeed, it felt good to be rushed as I sailed past a flotilla of scallop boats moored just off the ramp. At the Coast Guard station at Brant Point, a couple of guys were working on one of their boats. They looked up and waved.

At the base of the East Jetty is a gap for boats to cut through on their way toward Great Point. My plan was to sail through the cut to escape the incoming tide and follow the jetty all the way out, then head back through the harbor entrance. I hoped I could make the circuit in under an hour and, of course, see some seals along the way.

The tide was very low. After grounding on a shoal and having to jump out and drag the boat clear, I sailed through the cut. I'd never been this close to the jetty before. It was huge, a massive wall of boulders that radiated the same sense of man-made might that I had felt when walking the decks of an aircraft carrier. Humans might be puny, but we can sure make an impact; we can create worlds.

I sailed down this artificial peninsula of barnacled rocks where the waves slopped and slurped as ducks and gulls swam and preened. On a dead run with the boom pointed out toward Great Point, I could sail within a whisker of the jetty in my search for seals. When my rudder popped up on an unanticipated rock, I might have rounded up and crashed if a desperate roll to windward hadn't kept me on course until I had time to get the rudder back down.

It was then, after I'd pushed the rudder into position, that the rocks began to move. What I had taken for rocks were actually seals that were almost the same gray-brown color of the jetty and nearly six feet long. First they'd lift their heads and tails into the air and begin to rock like hobbyhorses before rolling their sausage-like bodies off the boulders and into the water on the other side of the jetty. Just ahead of me a small pup panicked, rolled the wrong way, and plopped into the water beside me. As I watched him skitter away, I discovered that a group of seals was following me, about fifteen yards back.

By the time I reached the end of the East Jetty, where a lone harrier hawk presided over a flock of cormorants drying their wings in the cold December sun, I had left this first group of seals behind. But I had hopes of finding more of them on the West Jetty. The wind was perfect for sailing upwind, just enough so that I could sit out on the deck and even hike out a little bit in a puff. Even though it was only three o'clock in the afternoon, the sun was already low in the sky, and the mast cast a shadow across the yellow light filling the sail.

I sailed to the buoy just off the West Jetty, which I had rounded in very different conditions on my way to Capaum Pond, and maneuvered so that I was heading directly toward the jetty. Suddenly the entire sweep of the jetty came alive with seals, rocking and then rolling into the harbor. This time, however, they remained on my side of the jetty, swimming underneath my boat and then popping up behind me.

At first I had a difficult time figuring out where they were going to appear next. Finally I realized they were operating as a unit. If I sailed into the midst of them they would inevitably reassemble behind me. In order to stay as close as possible to them, I began sailing in large circles, swooping back toward them after they had dived underneath the boat.

Once they understood that I didn't bite, they began lingering longer and longer, extending their heads a few feet above the water, until I was almost on top of them. We all seemed to be thoroughly enjoying ourselves.

I soon realized that I had only fifteen minutes to get back to Children's Beach. Reluctantly I tacked up the channel with the tide pushing me along. It was the first time since I'd started my training that I'd had what I considered to be the ideal breeze—light enough to use my body weight to control the heel of the boat but not so light that I was forced to sit in the cockpit. The boat began to feel like an extension of my body, a thing to be manipulated, not driven or hung on to. This was the feeling that had been missing all fall, a sense of the boat as an alive and ethereal being, the rudder and mainsheet parts of an interactive game with the sea and sky. D. H. Lawrence had described it: "Beautifully the sailing ship nodalizes the forces of sea and wind, converting them to her purpose. There is no violation . . . only a winged centrality. It is this perfect equipoise between them and us, which gives us a great part of our life-joy." Lawrence clearly knew the Zone.

Sailors have a word to describe the sensitivity required to achieve "this perfect equipoise"; it's called feel, and to a certain extent either you have it or you don't. I've seen a professional baseball player, a superb athlete with absolutely no feel, become so disoriented during a routine day sail that he slipped and fell out of a boat.

I've seen a fifty-eight-year-old woman with a bad hip step into the same sailboat that gave the baseball player such trouble and be immediately at home. Instead of unnerving her, the unsteadiness of the water and the flukiness of the breeze liberated her from the cruel grasp of dry land and gravity that forced her to walk with a cane. She intuitively understood and was delighted by the way sailing reinvented the playing field. The athlete, on the other hand, wanted no part of it.

More than anything else, feel is a matter of empathy with wind and water. Whereas most sports deny nature altogether, a sailor cannot escape it. As long as the wind fills the sails, he or she is consorting with a force beyond human control. But feel doesn't emanate from a higher, spiritual plane. On the contrary, it is primitive, elemental. Feel reaches back into the marrow and the synapses, into the brine of the bloodstream. Everything is reduced to instinct. As I sail, I am a throwback to an earlier evolutionary stage; I am very like a seal.

On that December afternoon as I sailed around Brant Point, I owed the seals a debt of gratitude. With their help I had begun to feel once again like a sailor.

PART II
This Is Only a Test

There are certain queer times and occasions in this strange mixed affair we call life when a man takes this whole universe for a vast practical joke, though the wit thereof he but dimly discerns, and more than suspects that the joke is at nobody's expense but his own.... That odd sort of wayward mood I am speaking of, comes over a man only in some time of extreme tribulation; it comes in the very midst of his earnestness, so that what just before might have seemed to him a thing most momentous, now seems but a part of a general joke.

—HERMAN MELVILLE, *Moby-Dick*

Details

Beginning with the Hundred Year Storm in December and continuing until the end of February, a string of fourteen consecutive three-day nor'easters buffeted the island, so that when the ponds weren't frozen, the conditions were virtually unsailable. Still, before the Midwinters in March I was able to get in two cursory, cold, and, for the most part, unsatisfactory sails. The first one was on the waters of Hummock, a long and lean pond extending down from Head of Hummock to the south shore of the island. Where Head of Hummock had been a hamster wheel, Hummock itself had been a flurry of tacks between two converging shores. Then there was Long Pond, a narrow squiggle of brackish water on the western end of the island that served as the boundary between a housing development and the mountainous town dump.

Perhaps it was just as well that I had only two more chances to sail before the Midwinters. By February I had begun to panic about the equipment I needed if I was going to be competitive in Sarasota. A lot had happened to the class since I had last raced in a regatta. A new, larger sail had been adopted, and other modifications had been legalized to make steering and hiking out easier. New ways of rigging the boat made it much easier to adjust the shape of the sail.

I was terrified. The Sunfish that I had known and loved was now a different boat. Why did I wait till I was on the verge of my first regatta before I began to update my equipment? In my heart of hearts I had held to a conviction that the changes were fairly superficial. Certainly the new sail would take some getting used to, but a Sunfish should be a Sunfish. By the middle of February I began to realize the price of denial.

Using a Sunfish rigging and tuning guide that had been recently reprinted in the class newsletter, I assembled the equipment that I would need to prepare the boat I was chartering in Sarasota. Over the next few weeks a green duffel bag dating back to my college days began to fill up with line, blocks, tools, and duct tape. I sent away to the class headquarters in Michigan for some sail numbers and applied my old, tried-and-true number 47036 to a stiff, crackly new sail.

Besides chartering a boat for the regatta, I also had to find accommodations. One of the regatta organizers found me a free place to sleep on a cruising sailboat kept in a nearby slip. Then there was the plane ticket and the rent-a-car, and suddenly it was 8:00 a.m. on a Thursday in March and I was saying good-bye to Melissa and the kids.

I wasn't prepared for the overpowering sense of guilt that

swept over me after walking Jennie and Ethan to their bus stop. I'll never forget their sad, hurt looks as they waved to me through the side window before the old yellow bus lurched into gear and was gone.

At the airport Melissa could tell I was having second thoughts about the trip. "You okay?" she asked.

"Why am I doing this?" I blurted.

"You're asking me?"

"I'm going to get my ass kicked. I'm not going to know anybody. It's going to cost too much—"

"Forget about the sailing, just enjoy being in Florida. You need a break."

I smiled wanly and nodded.

"And Nat," she said with a coy, girlish grin that dated back to the early days of our relationship when we developed our own nautical variation of the old Broadway good-luck line, "break a stay."

Soon the commuter plane to Boston was giving me a bird's-eye view of the island and its ponds. There they were: Gibbs, Sesachacha, Coskata, Miacomet, Head of Hummock and Hummock, Long, Capaum, and, of course, the Creeks. I remembered the time I'd seen someone experiencing a similar view of Nantucket's ponds. I'd just pulled into a parking lot at Sanford Farm overlooking Hummock and Head of Hummock ponds. Walking painfully up a nearby hill was a friend of mine, a local sailor reaching the end of a battle with cancer. His body looked as if it had been crushed, and yet there he stood, gazing out over a wide valley and a necklace of ponds that stretched to the sea. After less than a minute, he turned and started down the hill to his car. At the time I'd hoped the ponds had provided him with a momentary distraction from all the pain and dread. But deep down I knew differently. Instead of seeking relief, he had climbed this hill to say good-bye.

A Different World

On the plane from Boston to Sarasota the in-flight movie was *Forever Young*. When not watching Mel Gibson turn into an old man, I spent the flight attempting to get a grip on my doubts about Sarasota. If I wasn't prepared as a sailor, at least I could be ready as a historian, and I pored over a small pile of books and pamphlets sent by my in-laws, who'd recently bought a condominium near there. On a map the area bore a distinct resemblance to Coatue, the peninsula along the outer edge of Nantucket Harbor. Nantucket's historical heyday ended in the mid-nineteenth century, just as Sarasota's was beginning.

A handful of Scots were the first Europeans to make a go of the place, building what some claim to be the country's first golf course. By 1920 Sarasota was poised to take off, transforming itself almost overnight from a sleepy three-thousand-person fishing town into a hopping resort of more than eight thousand by 1925. Sarasota marketed itself brilliantly to northerners, calling itself the place "where summer spends the winter." The chamber of commerce even had its own radio station that could be heard as far away as Chicago. As many a northerner bought and sold land that he had never even seen, prices in Sarasota went through the roof.

I was familiar with the scenario. When we had first moved to Nantucket in 1986, the island was in the grip of just this kind of real estate feeding frenzy. Property values were increasing by 25 percent a year. A person would buy a lot in the morning and sell it by that afternoon and make a 30 percent profit, a process that came to be known as "flipping." And just as had happened on Nantucket in the late eighties, Sarasota busted as quickly as it had boomed.

But in the early sixties the cycle began again. Developers moved in, transforming the keys along the edge of Sarasota Bay into a series of beachside resorts. In 1950 fewer than thirty thousand people had lived there; by 1980 there were nearly seven times that many.

Things certainly looked prosperous as I drove down the long causeway that connects Sarasota to its keys. The roads were clean and newly painted, full of white rental cars. The quality of the light was entirely different from New England's. There was something dreamy and ethereal about the blue-green waters and the sugar-white sand. The pelicans, egrets, and sandpipers looked more like special effects from Disney than things of this world.

Halfway down the causeway, I began to notice sailboats— a fleet of Sunfish returning from a practice race. There must have been twenty, maybe thirty boats out there. When I had sailed in my one and only Midwinters in 1979, it had been a most informal and sparsely attended affair. Now, fourteen years later, there were more Sunfish sailing a practice race on Sarasota Bay than had attended the entire 1979 event.

A light-to-moderate breeze was blowing, and the watery, otherworldly quality of the scene—bobbing boats with white sails gliding over an aquamarine sea—had a devastating effect on me. Those Sunfish out there looked so much more grace-ful, so much faster than they had in my youth. The regatta hadn't even started yet, and I already felt like a has-been about to make a landlubberly fool of himself.

Soon I was bouncing down a sandy path that snaked its way through a ragged field full of bleached-out sailboats. The race headquarters, the Sarasota Sailing Squadron, was a brick bunker amid the palms, so small and nondescript that I initially passed it by. Sunfish, some with their sails still up, were scattered around the lawn and docks. Many were just arriving on car roofs and trailers. It was already late after-noon, and with darkness fast approaching, I needed to de-vote as much time as possible to preparing my chartered boat for tomorrow. Not far from the clubhouse I found my boat. The hull had been used only once before, at a recent World Championship in Aruba. Since I had brought my old, trusty daggerboard and rudder with me and fittings were already in place for the other modifications I needed to make, most of what I had to do that evening involved at-taching my brand-new sail to the spars.

I was eager for all the help I could get, and a local ace named Jeff Linton took the time to show me how to create a

system that made adjusting sail shape a thing of almost fin-
gertip control. Although Jeff couldn't have been more helpful, I was feeling less like a champion and more like Rip Van
Winkle. In the last decade and a half, not only had the Sunfish become more high-tech, the scene around the parking
lot had also changed. Vans with logos on them were everywhere with all sorts of stuff to sell, from hats to tiller extensions to sunblock. Since I was fast discovering that I hadn't
brought everything I needed, it was great to have the equivalent of a marine hardware store at the regatta site. None-
theless, it was a much more commercial scene than in the
old days. As night came on, I retreated into the fluorescent
glow of the clubhouse to register and find out where I was
going to be sleeping that night.

Inside, the Sarasota Sailing Squadron was as unpreten-
tious as it was on the outside. The floor was poured concrete.
There was a television, a drinking fountain, and a bar and
grill where you could buy a beer and a hot dog for a dollar
each. This was definitely a sailing club that had its priorities
straight.

I soon met Cindy and Charlie Clifton, two locals who had
helped organize the regatta. They immediately impressed me
as people I wanted to get to know. Their teenage son was an
up-and-coming junior champ, and their daughter was a track
star on the verge of college. A warm and welcoming sailing
family, they reminded me of my own.

Although my parents had not been as outgoing, they had
created a similar environment for my brother and me once it
had become clear that sailing was to be our destiny. At first

they simply drove my brother Sam and me to regatta after regatta. Then, soon after I got my driver's license, they bought two boats of their own, and we were a family of four Sunfish racers, often driving to regattas in convoy, each car trailing two Sunfish behind. It was great to see that this tradition was still alive in the nineties.

My home away from home turned out to be *Spars and Bars*, a thirty-foot racing sloop that had been dismasted a while ago and now appeared to function mainly as a floating dormitory for visiting sailors. After reserving one of the bunks with my duffel bag, I spent a pleasant hour reintroducing myself to a dizzying assortment of friends from the old days, then had dinner at a glitzy fern bar nearby. By midnight I was back on *Spars and Bars*, where I lay wide awake for more than an hour, drinking in the sensations of this semitropical night: the rhythmic beat of halyards against masts, the slurp of wavelets against the hull's side, and the rustling of palm trees in the wind. It dawned on me that this was going to be the longest I'd been away from home since Jennie's birth, more than ten years ago. It was about time I'd done something like this, I told myself over and over again until finally I fell asleep.

Into the Maelstrom

I AWOKE LATER THAN I had wanted. When I emerged from *Spars and Bars*, the Sailing Squadron's parking lot and lawn were bustling with activity. Boats were being unloaded, sails raised, old friends were shaking hands and slapping backs.

I had about an hour before I had to leave the beach. Soon I was off in the far corner of the club lawn and fiddling with my sail. These new sails were different. Besides having a fuller and more powerful shape, they were made out of heavier, more durable cloth. By the time I headed for the clubhouse to fill my water bottle, I wished I had arrived a day earlier just to sort out the new variables.

The bulletin board announced that 104 boats had registered for the regatta, making it the biggest Midwinters on record. This was a long way from sailing by myself on a pond on Nantucket. I was making my way through the crowded parking lot when a white Lincoln Continental with a Sunfish on the roof pulled up and parked right in front of me.

Through the tinted windshield I could dimly see that the driver was waving at me. It turned out to be Alan Scharfe, an old friend with whom I had roomed at the Sunfish Worlds in Puerto Rico in 1978. At one point during that regatta the two of us were in the hotel elevator on our way to dinner. Suddenly the elevator lurched to a stop, and for the next hour we were trapped in a tiny, humid, and very hot box. The highlight of our confinement occurred when the hotel custodian told us "Don't go anywhere" while he went for help. Over the last fifteen years I'd seen Alan a handful of times, and each time one of us inevitably retold that story.

Now a successful electrical contractor in the Boston area, Alan, despite a laid-back, affable manner, was a top-notch racer who regularly finished in the top five of the world championships. As I helped him unload his boat, he asked where I was staying. It turned out he had booked a room in the Holiday Inn at nearby Lido Key, and he offered me his room's sleeper sofa.

"Hey," I said enthusiastically, "it'll be just like the Worlds in Puerto Rico!"

Alan smiled. "Yeah, remember that time when we got stuck in the elevator. . . ."

It was a perfect day for a sailboat race, with blue skies and a ten-to-twelve-knot breeze. The massed fleet heading for the starting line looked like a giant flock of migrating birds. There were Sunfish ahead of me, Sunfish behind me, Sunfish on every side. I was awestruck and slightly baffled. A horn sounded and a yellow flag rose—ten minutes before the start. My watch had hands instead of a digital display, making it difficult to keep track of how many minutes I had left. In an instant I felt the full impact of my unpreparedness.

What made it all the worse was the memory of how it used to be. Instead of a blur of boats, I used to see a fleet of individual competitors. Instead of wallowing in aimless confusion, I had studied the fleet like Nelson, assessing every possible advantage. I had been in command. Now I was just an ordinary seaman.

With one minute to go, I was so jacked up on adrenaline that I could barely hold the tiller. I saw a hole on the leeward end of the starting line, opposite the committee boat, and went for it. I trimmed in the sail and then—no starting gun. I had screwed up the time. There was still one minute to go. So there I was, in the worst possible position. I had already crossed the starting line and now I had only a few precious seconds to find a place on a starting line that was already jam-packed. As I jibed around the buoy end, I saw nothing but boats.

By the time the actual starting gun fired, I was back in the third row. This was not how I'd envisioned my first regatta. The first row of boats jumped out and were off, leaving the rest of us to find some leftover wind. No matter where I went, there was always a boat almost directly ahead of me, its sail sucking away my air. I was mired in the back of the fleet, unable to pass the kind of people I used to eat for breakfast and even being passed by some of them.

One elderly gentleman with a wide-brim hat and a Hawaiian shirt was particularly annoying. Here I was in my state-of-the-art lifejacket, boots, and sailing gloves, *looking* like I should be going fast, and yet, dammit, this joker was making me look like a fool. After we traded tacks for the last half of the beat, he rounded the windward mark just ahead of me.

It was an ego-shattering experience. All my fears, worries, and insecurities came bubbling to the surface. This was exactly the nightmare I had hoped to avoid. In the distance ahead, the leaders were anonymous speedsters, masters of skills that were now beyond me. Then I began to notice that along with the guy in the hat and Hawaiian shirt, there were more than a few young bucks in my vicinity. I wasn't the only guy in the back of the pack wearing an expensive lifejacket.

I eventually finished fifty-fifth, smack-dab in the middle of the fleet. Going into this regatta, I had dared to think that I might be able to at least challenge the leaders. At this point, I wasn't even in their league; I couldn't even see who they were.

The next race was considerably better: I finished in twenty-fifth place. Still, I had no sense of mastery or accomplishment. I had no sense for what was happening with the wind shifts. Instead of thinking two tacks ahead, I was reacting to situations that I should never have allowed to develop. I had made two mistakes that required me to sail penalty circles. My sailing was messy and out of control. As I sailed back to the club, I thought seriously about catching an early flight back to Nantucket.

It didn't get any better when Alan, who'd finished a

respectable seventh in the first race, greeted me at the score-board inside the club by asking, "What happened?"

"Isn't it obvious?" I wanted to snarl. "I suck!" But after taking a deep breath, I tried, as best I could, to explain what had indeed happened.

Roll Call

I BEGAN TO CLIMB out of my Slough of Despond that evening as Alan and others introduced me to the current breed of Sunfish sailors. The fastest sailor of the day had been Bob Findlay, who had amassed an impressive record over the years, winning the Midwinters a total of five times while also doing well in Laser and Hobie Cat championships. Of my generation, with a wife and a couple of kids, Bob was proof that having a family and winning major Sunfish regattas were not mutually exclusive.

The Midwinters was dominated by the presence of master (over forty years of age) sailors, who accounted for more than half the fleet. In addition to these "confirmed" master sailors, there was a large group of "emerging" masters—sailors my age or slightly older who had either stuck with it all these years or were, like me, just getting back into it.

I began to attach names to all those anonymous boats, and what struck me was the remarkable diversity of the Sunfish class. Most singlehanded classes are raced by strong young men in their twenties. For example, racing the Laser competitively with a full sail in a decent breeze requires a body weight of at least 165 pounds and excellent physical conditioning. The Sunfish, however, is a different animal. Thanks to its chines, its hull shape is more stable than that of the round-sided Laser. The Sunfish's untraditional rig, while it may look strange, is efficient and adaptable enough to allow lighter-weight women and children to remain competitive, even in high winds. There is no other sailboat as inexpensive and light as the Sunfish that can be effectively raced by such a wide range of people.

At the Midwinters there would be eight master sailors and four women in the top twenty; the top junior (sixteen years and under) would finish twenty-third. Those gathered around the keg at the Sarasota Sailing Squadron that Friday evening were the kind of people you might see at a community barbecue—fathers, mothers, kids, single professionals, not to mention plenty of grandmothers and grandfathers.

After moving out of *Spars and Bars*, I followed Alan to the Holiday Inn. He had a spectacular top-floor room overlooking the Gulf of Mexico. That night we had dinner together at the hotel restaurant, and Alan, a newly retired Sunfish Class president, filled me in on the class's recent history.

The eighties had been tough on the Sunfish and on sailing in general. What had been a truly grassroots sport in the sixties and seventies began to lose people right and left. Many young kids traded traditional "sit down" classes like the Sunfish and Laser for "stand up" craft known as sailboards or

Windsurfers. Other sailors traded in their sailboats for motorboats because they were easier to use and didn't require a
crew. More than a few sailboat manufacturers went bankrupt.
AMF, the giant conglomerate that had bought out Alcort,
the Sunfish's original builder, back in the seventies, decided
to get out of the boat business.

Although attendance at major championships had dimin-
ished throughout the 1980s, the Sunfish was now, according to Alan, poised for a comeback. For one thing, the class
had a new and committed builder. For another, pockets of
regional activity had demonstrated remarkable strength in
recent years. While New England, once the stronghold of
the class, had begun to fade from the forefront, the Midwest
and especially the Southeast were stronger than ever. This
Midwinters' attendance by "Team Florida" from the state's
west coast was particularly impressive. And finally, there
were baby boomers like me who were finding their way back
to the boat of their youth. That night on the sofa bed, I began
to think about the day I'd just had and the day that lay ahead.
Even though I had experienced a past champion's worst
nightmare, perhaps it was for the best. Certainly, I assured
myself, it couldn't get any worse.

Over Early

Sailing out to the course the next morning differed completely from the day before. For one thing, I'd begun to recognize the people I had known in the old days, and it was startling to realize that they still sailed with the exact same posture of fifteen years ago. Things were beginning to seem almost familiar.

I had an okay start in the middle of the line. Nothing inspired, but sufficient. The wind was lighter than the day before, and it would continue to drop throughout the race. Although I was a long way back from the leaders, I wasn't completely out of touch, and I made a point of watching them as they rounded the leeward mark at the end of the first triangle. I wanted to learn anything that might prove useful.

Once again it was Bob Findlay in the lead. He was immediately recognizable as the person who moved the most in his boat. Even though the wind was relatively light and he was barely able to sit out on the deck, he was constantly jumping around his boat and adjusting the mainsheet.

Watching Bob made it clear that I was still a relative stick-in-the-mud. While most of us were just sitting there, Bob was a virtual perpetual motion machine, and yet there was a subtlety, even a delicacy, to his movements. This guy was going to be very tough to beat in Springfield.

I ended up finishing twenty-second. Not great, but my best finish to date. It turned out I was in good company, amid a cluster of past champions and contenders. This was a very tough fleet. There was no reason for despair.

Eventually the breeze died down to a near dead calm. For the next few hours we waited for wind and ate lunches provided by a support boat. For the most part, I hung out with Alan. It was very companionable, bobbing there side by side on windless Sarasota Bay with our legs sprawled across the decks of our Sunfish as we lay back in our cockpits, our tiller extensions resting on our shoulders, and talked. All the gabbing had a soothing, revivifying effect. By the time the wind had risen to the point that the race committee felt they could attempt another start, I had decided that this was going to be my race.

Others seemed to have the same idea. As time wound down for the start, it became obvious that a large portion of the fleet was going to be over the line early. The race committee was forced to recall the fleet and begin again. This had already happened a few times before, and the race committee raised a black flag to indicate that any boat venturing over the line with less than a minute to go before the next start would be automatically disqualified. This had the desired effect, and the start proceeded without a hitch.

I nailed a magnificent start on the windward end of the line. It was the kind of start I used to manage on a fairly regular basis. How different things seemed from up here on the edge of the fleet! Now it wasn't a question of clearing my air; now it was a question of consolidating my position up here in the stratosphere. I was walking across a high wire; one misstep and I would tumble down into the fleet below me.

Should I tack, or should I keep going and try to stay with the rest of the fleet? I began to panic, but in an entirely different way from that first race the day before. In a certain sense it was a kind of stage fright. Here I was, caught in the spotlight, and what was I supposed to do? I told myself that the secret was not to try too hard. Regattas weren't won by being brilliant. No, they were won by not messing up. I should sit back, go fast, and let the rest of the fleet make the moves, positioning myself so as to minimize any potential damage from wayward wind shifts. I must clear my head and go with the percentage move. I didn't need to be first; I just needed a decent finish.

Unfortunately it was an awfully big course, and from my starting point over on the committee boat end, it was difficult to keep in touch with those who had started over on the leeward end of the line. And as fate would have it, the other side of the course ended up paying off. Still, I ended up fourteenth. On the way back to the club I was jubilant.

As I approached the club I could hear the throbbing bass of a rock band warming up for the regatta party scheduled for that evening. My in-laws, Marshall and Betty Douthart, were on the pier videotaping the fleet as it sailed into the club. On the tape I at least look like one of the fast guys—the sail low and boom cocked up at a rakish angle, my sunglasses giving me a vaguely threatening appearance—Pondman goes tropical. The best part of the video shows a great mass of boats well behind me.

After a brief chat with my in-laws, I made my way to the scoreboard. Alan was already there. He was shaking his head. When he saw me, he laughed and slapped me on the back.

"Join the club," he said.

Instead of having just scored my best finish of the regatta, I'd scored my worst. I had been over the starting line early in the fourth race, and as a result I'd been disqualified, adding more than one hundred points to my score. Even if we were allowed to throw out our worst race, which would happen if seven races were completed, I'd have to count my horrible first race. As it stood, I was in fiftieth overall.

But Alan helped me put it into perspective. He had also been a victim of the black flag, not once but twice. We couldn't believe it. Weren't the hotshot young kids supposed to be the ones who were called over early?

After I'd gotten over the shock of what it had done to my cumulative score, I almost began to enjoy the fact that I'd been over early. It was a badge of honor. "How'd you do?" someone would ask. "Over early in the fourth," I'd reply with a knowing smile. It was like getting caught for speeding on the highway—the price of living on the edge, being footloose in the fast lane.

I was able to sustain this macho denial for only a few beers. By the time I returned to the hotel for a shower, I was cursing myself for pushing it at that start. There had been no need. But tomorrow would be another day, and now I had nothing to lose.

What Ifs

As we sailed out to the course on Sunday, I felt numb. Here I was, into my third and last day of the Midwinters and I was in the precise middle of the fleet. Two months earlier, I would have been horrified at the thought. So why didn't I even seem to care?

The wind was light. Since they wanted to sail three races, the race committee got things off quickly. I managed a reasonable start in the middle of the line and came in twentieth.

The next race marked the first time that I felt like I might be able to sail at my old level. I finished eighth and was, for a change, not losing boats toward the end. Bob Findlay won, virtually assuring him the regatta win, and the race committee decided to go for one more.

My expectations were high, but at this stage I just didn't have what it took to break into the top five. I finished fifteenth. Once again, it was not a bad showing in relation to the overall standings, but it was not the phenomenal finish I had been yearning for.

After packing away all my stuff and venturing back to the clubhouse, I was astonished to see that my day's racing had taken me from fiftieth to twentieth overall! I did a few "what if" calculations. If I hadn't been over early in the fourth race, I'd have ended up around twelfth overall. If I had maintained my third-day average throughout the series, I'd have cracked the top ten.

I'd been through a three-day process of spiritual breakdown and reconstruction, a necessary catharsis if I was going to approach the North Americans in four months with any hope of doing well. I now had a whole new laundry list of goals and objectives, and above all, I now realized that the ponds on Nantucket, each with its own peculiar demands, were very appropriate practice waters. It was not strength and endurance I needed, but sensitivity and smarts.

Unfortunately, Alan was not going to be able to sail in the North Americans. We both agreed that seeing each other had been the highlight of our Midwinters. Neither one of us had done as well as we had hoped, but as Alan reminded me, "This time we didn't get stuck in an elevator."

PART III

The Swift Monster

For as the swift monster drags you deeper and deeper into the frantic shoal, you bid adieu to circumspect life and only exist in a delirious throb.
—HERMAN MELVILLE, *Moby-Dick*

Oedipal Sailing

It took me a while, but gradually I began to figure out that most of my problems in Florida had had little to do with sailing and a lot to do with me. It wasn't until I'd been home for a few weeks and was back into writing the book that I realized just how out of whack I'd been in Sarasota.

It all came down to family. Without my wife and kids, I'd been a wire stripped of its casing; I'd been a "primary caregiver" who was no longer primary and hardly without a care. I'd been a basket case.

I thought back to that blessed event—the 1978 Sunfish North Americans—which still loomed so large across the years. It had been sailed in Barrington, Rhode Island, the same little town in which my father had summered as a boy. Our family had spent the week of the races in my grandmother's summer home, a wonderful and familiar little place less than ten minutes from the regatta site. Instead of being a lone wolf in the wilderness, I'd had the ultimate support system, enabling me to unwind each night within the warm and welcoming bosom of my family. Looking back, I wondered whether I'd won the regatta not because I was the best sailor but because I'd had Mom to cook dinner for me every night.

The more I thought about it, the more I realized that sailing had always been inextricably tied to family, and any attempt to separate the two would be like setting up a Berlin Wall across the interior of my brain. But how in God's name was I going to convince Melissa, Jennie, and Ethan to come to Springfield, Illinois, in July?

It was Sunday, March 21. It had been two weeks since I'd returned from Florida, and I was deep within, if not the bosom of my family, at least the interior of my parents' car, driving down Route 6 on Cape Cod in a dank, Stinker-like vehicle full of sailboat equipment. Melissa and the kids were attending Jennie's swim team finals at Massachusetts Maritime Academy. I'd been granted a reprieve so I could sail with my parents, who were now retired and living just across Nantucket Sound near Hyannis, the mainland ferry terminus that is to Nantucket what my parents had once been to me—the source of supply, the lifeline to the world.

I'd always assumed my parents would go the way of most sailors; that they'd move on to bigger and more comfortable boats as they entered their golden years. Instead they turned to the six-foot-four-inch Cape Cod Frosty, which, in addition to being the smallest racing class in the world, is (as the name might suggest) sailed only in the off-season. The Frosty is an absurd matchbox of a boat that forces an adult sailor to become a contortionist just to fit into it. After an hour, both knees are on fire and the back throbs. But for masochists it's fun, and since my parents had an extra boat, I decided to go Frosty sailing. Besides, in the Philbrick family the best way to visit is if a sailboat of some kind is involved.

So with two boats on the trailer, one on the roof, and me stuck in a backseat jammed with sails, rudders, and other equipment, we headed for Wychmere Harbor, a tiny anchorage in Harwichport. My parents are nothing if not punctual, and we were the first ones there. It was a gray, rainy, light-air day, and soon the rest of the fleet began to arrive.

This was the first race day of the spring season, and a series of winter storms had inflicted its share of damage on the Wychmere race committee "boat," a little dock-mounted shack that had had its roof and windows blown off. Fortunately, the section of roof and even the window were found on a nearby shore, and with the help of a hammer and nails, repairs were effected in a matter of minutes.

There were ten of us, including "Poppa Frosty," Tom Leach, the Harwichport harbormaster who had invented the boat back in the early eighties. Tim O'Keeffe, a past Frosty North American champion, was also part of the group, but with many of the fleet having the last name of Philbrick, this was destined to be something of a family affair.

In the old days my mother had always been a relatively reluctant sailor. Traumatic memories from her youth (her father used to yell at her through a bullhorn when she raced her Beetle Cat) kept sailing from being her first love. My father, on the other hand, had been a champion sailor, and as a young parent he had taken to Sunfish racing with obvious relish. In fact, in my adolescent days, when I was going through all sorts of hormone-induced tirades, I developed a mental block when it came to racing against my dad. Even though I had progressed to the point that I should have been able to beat him relatively easily, I always seemed to mess up if the two of us were on the same race course. I'd find myself unnecessarily obsessing about where he was, and sure enough, Pop would always end up passing me at the finish.

Eventually my brother and I moved into the "470," a two-person, Olympic-class boat, and then came college. When I came back to the Sunfish during the summer of my junior year, I was pleased to discover that my father phobia had passed. I could now sail in the same race with him and not find myself constantly looking over my shoulder.

I will always remember one race in particular during the Sunfish North Americans in Barrington. It was early in the series, and I was fighting it out for first overall. Both my father and my brother were in the championship fleet. The wind had built up to twenty knots. I was in my element; my father, a light-air expert but definitely no heavy-air animal, was out of his. We had already sailed three races that day, and one more was scheduled. The fleet was lining up for the start. I was planing down the line, looking for a hole. I saw my opportunity and went for it, belatedly realizing that I was setting up to windward of my father.

So there we were, side by side with thirty seconds to go. I remember feeling several different emotions. First I felt a sense of reassurance. I knew that Pop must be totally exhausted; indeed, he was just the kind of guy I wanted to leeward of me because I knew I could grind him into the dust.

I also felt guilty. How could I trample all over my own father? And then as the seconds wound down, I found myself going through the same motions I would have gone through with anyone else, hitting the line at full speed, rounding up, and sailing over him almost immediately.

I won that race, and looking back, it was the race that turned the series around for me, giving me the confidence to hold off the competition until the bitter end. Pop and I have never talked about that start, but it still stands in my memory as the moment when I finally put all the tortured agony of my adolescence behind me.

In his retirement my dad has established an extremely consistent record in the Frosty. My mom, on the other hand, has always been a wild card. Sometimes she can surprise you, coming out of a far corner of the race course to finish unexpectedly well. Just as often she opts to remain onshore, reading in the car rather than getting rained on in a Frosty. This day, however, despite the occasional drizzle, she sailed all afternoon.

We sailed five races. Maintaining the bad habits I had acquired in Sarasota, I was over early in the last race, and finished third overall. The winner? My mom! She put us all to shame, combining blazing boat speed with smart, conservative tactics. After the second race (which she won), she sighed and announced, "Well, now I can die content." For "serious" racers such as my father and myself, my mom's carefree approach can be frustrating. While we were beating to the finish, and I was consumed with trying to catch a favorable shift on the left-hand side, she asked how my book was coming. By the end of the day I'd begun to suspect that my mother's questions were not as ingenuous as they at first appeared.

Perhaps the best race was the third, in which Mom, Pop, and I finished first, second, and third. At the awards ceremony held in a local bar, there were a lot of snide comments about that race, with several unsubstantiated accusations of team racing. Mom silenced the critics by ordering onion rings all around.

That night, after meeting up with Melissa and the kids at my parents' home, we took the late boat back to Nantucket. We'd brought our car with us, and since it was already 8:30 we decided to stay below on the freight deck rather than venture up to the passenger section. As Melissa read in the passenger seat, and Jennie, Ethan, and Molly the dog slept behind us, I scribbled notes about my day of Frosty sailing.

Pop was too honest to be entirely gracious in defeat; although he had been pleased by Mom's performance, he couldn't help but be disappointed that he hadn't done better (he finished fifth), and he'd talked about making changes to his Frosty's hull. I thought about how my love of sailing and my career as a writer could all be traced in various ways to my father, a retired English professor whose specialty is James Fenimore Cooper and American maritime literature. Only then did I realize how early I'd begun to soak up his passion for racing sailboats.

When my brother and I were very young, Pop told us a bedtime story that I have never forgotten. My father's older brother Charlie had been a fierce competitor in the Beetle

Cat class, ultimately winning the junior championship in 1939. Charlie would go on to become a fighter pilot in World War II, then a prizewinning poet before dying of cancer at a tragically early age. For my father, Charlie would always embody a swashbuckling, win-at-all-costs recklessness that on a summer day in the late 1930s almost got him killed.

The morning began with a flat calm, and figuring that he wanted the lightest crew he could find, Charlie decided that his younger brother Tommy, not even ten years old, should sail with him. The race began with light enough winds, but inevitably the sea breeze started to build. It wasn't long before Charlie and his pipsqueak crew were hopelessly overpowered. But Charlie, cursing and cajoling, pushed on. My father was terrified.

Then, in the midst of the race, a wave brought them down on the submerged tip of a stake marking an oyster bed. Even though it punched a hole into the boat's wooden bottom, Charlie wasn't about to give up. Ripping off his shirt, he insisted that little Tommy stuff it into the hole and hold it there. As water bubbled into the boat and my father tossed from side to side within the sloshing confines beneath the Beetle Cat's deck, Charlie sailed his sinking ship on. Remarkably, they finished the race in second, but for Charlie it had been a disaster. They hadn't won, and it was all Tommy's fault.

Unlike my mother, who knew enough to tell her father to go to hell when it came to racing sailboats, my father followed in his charismatic brother's footsteps despite, or perhaps because of, the early trauma he had experienced. My father is one of the sanest men I have ever known, except when it comes to sailing. It inspires in him, as it does in me, a Charlie-like frenzy, a state of madness in which all the passions we otherwise dare not express spill forth.

Sailing has always been for the Philbrick family a competitive endeavor, and I now wondered whether on the starting line of that pivotal race in the Sunfish North Americans I had unconsciously assumed the role of Charlie, the dominating and remorseless older brother.

Leaving Hyannis that night, deep within the belly of the ferry headed for our Nantucket home, I wrote: "Pop is a guy whom I greatly admire and try to emulate and, ultimately, try to beat. There, I said it."

The Prop

Iᴛ ᴡᴀs sᴘʀɪɴɢ, and I was back to sailing Nantucket's ponds. With the Midwinters behind me, I discovered I had a very different approach. This was now less a cosmic journey into the bleak kettle holes of my soul and more a weekly practice session for an upcoming regatta, a regatta that was now only three months away.

The day was cold and gray, a throwback to winter, as I drove out toward Madaket with Melissa and the kids. Across the street from Long Pond was Head of Long Pond, a roundish open pool that seemed suitable for a no-nonsense hour of training. I knew the weaknesses I needed to work on: mark roundings, tacking, and jibing—the essentials of boat handling. I also knew that I lacked the "one-with-the-boat" sensitivity that only time on the water can ingrain.

This time I had a prop—an old Clorox bottle tied to the head of a pickax. When I threw the rusted piece of iron into the Head of Long Pond, the clothesline following it down and the white buoy bobbing on the gray water, I felt a new sense of purpose. Gone were the days of relatively aimless exploration; now I had a focal point around which to organize my training session.

I practiced leeward mark roundings. Over and over again I approached the Clorox bottle on a run, working out the precise angle required to bring me within a whisker of the buoy as I headed up onto a beat. I performed rapid-fire tacking and jibing drills, to the point that I began to sweat. By the time I returned to shore, where Melissa and the kids waited in the car, I felt I had made a small but measurable advance toward preparing for the North Americans.

And yet something was wrong. I had been on my pond and they had been in the car. I could see what lay ahead: The more focused I became in the succeeding weeks, the more isolated I would become. If this comeback was going to count toward anything, it would have to somehow involve Melissa, Jennie, and Ethan.

Unfortunately, the last thing they wanted to do was tag along to Springfield. Unless you are participating in it, there is nothing more boring than a sailboat regatta, particularly one held outside a midwestern city in July.

But I had an alternative plan, a plan made possible by the demise of the Stinker only the week before. In its place was a brand-new Jeep Cherokee with a trailer hitch.

"Melissa," I said.

"Yes?" She glanced at me as we took the turn past a monument marking the birthplace of Abiah Folger, Benjamin Franklin's mother.

"How about the four of us sail in the Connecticut River Race?"

I had expected an incredulous laugh. Instead she said, "When is it?"

"Sometime in early June."

"What is it, exactly?"

"A two-day trip from Hartford to Essex, Connecticut. Two people per Sunfish. You camp overnight, so you've got to bring all your gear. My impression is that it's more of a voyage than it is a race."

"Where'd we get the second boat?"

"Sam says we can have his."

"How'd we get there?"

"We'd put both boats on the Beetle Cat trailer."

Melissa looked over her shoulder at the kids. So far her face had betrayed no emotion. By this point we were at the stop sign near the old Quaker Graveyard, a stoneless, rolling field of closely cropped grass.

"Jennie, Ethan, what do you think?"

Since they hadn't been listening very closely, we had to reintroduce the proposal. When Ethan heard there was camping involved he was all for it. Jennie wasn't as enthusiastic but seemed amenable.

We pulled into the parking space beside our house and sat in the car talking. All sorts of logistical problems had to be worked out, but none of them seemed insurmountable. At last Melissa nodded and said, "Let's do it."

Pre-Cut

In the spring I became something of a media darling, appearing in not only the local newspaper but also *Nantucket Magazine*. Early spring is a very slow news time on Nantucket. In fact, March is known on the island as "Hate Month." After a long winter of being cooped up, people start trading vicious rumors, and by the beginning of spring, the island is a tiny cauldron of scandal and suspicion. Any news—even a story about some guy sailing his way through a midlife crisis—is welcome news if it occurs in March. So after meeting a writer and a photographer on the shores of Miacomet Pond, I performed pirouettes out on the water and answered their questions. What had been a relatively secret quest was about to become public knowledge.

Since the island is surrounded by the cold ocean, spring is slow in coming to Nantucket. It wasn't until the first weekend in May, when I returned to Miacomet, that it felt as if winter was dead and gone and summer might not be too far away. People were fishing along the pond's banks; an assortment of canoes and tin fishing boats had fanned out across Miacomet's long and narrow confines. I was no longer alone.

After a half hour of mark-rounding drills in the southern extremity of the pond, which was so close to the ocean that I could hear the steady roar of waves, I decided to sail the pond's entire length, a dead beat that would provide excellent tacking practice. Soon I was tacking on an almost continual basis as the pond burrowed its way into a section of trees and marsh grass. It was like sailing in the midst of a forest. Ahead I could see three boys fishing. They seemed somewhat perplexed to see a sailboat coming their way. The youngest one shouted out, "Is sailing fun?"

"You bet," I said breathlessly. All the tacking was wearing me out. "But you know," I continued, "I think I'm about to run out of room."

Soon after I sailed past the boys' fishing lines, the pond petered out into a swampy section of marsh grass. The pond was too narrow, less than six feet, for me to turn around.

The boys and I talked for a while. They were fishing for perch but hadn't caught anything yet.

"Know what I'm going to do?" I said.

"No, what?"

"I'm going to sail out of here backwards."

"You can do that?"

"We'll see, but first you guys better pull in your lines so I don't run over them."

Sunfish are easy boats to sail backward. The trick is to hold the boom to the windward side so that the sail fills in from behind. With the rudder now at the front of the boat, steering is not only reversed but exceedingly sensitive.

Soon I was picking up speed in reverse, zooming past the kids in a kind of backward free fall. Given the narrowness of the pond, it felt almost like tumbling down an elevator shaft. Each little jerk of the tiller threatened to send me veering off into the pond bank, but I was able to keep the boat in the channel—a wild joyride in reverse that made me shout with excitement once the pond was wide enough to let me spin around and proceed in a forward direction down the pond. I turned and waved good-bye to the boys.

Two weeks later, on a Saturday in the middle of May, the weather was even warmer and sunnier. All four of us (plus the dog) went out to Clark's Cove, a pond that had once been part of Hummock before the ever-encroaching ocean to the south bit the pond in half, leaving the small part of what had been a J-shaped pond off by its lonesome. A field of lush green grass surrounded the pond, its brilliant blue waters sparkling in the sun. Beyond, only a few hundred yards to the south was the ocean, where fishing trawlers from New Bedford dragged their nets along the bottom. The scene was almost mesmerizing in its beauty—Big Sky openness with an island's intimacy.

A ten- to fifteen-knot breeze was blowing, and with my trusty pickax and Clorox bottle in the cockpit, I set out to perform my now customary drills. I'd been sailing for a good fifteen minutes when I noticed something swimming out in the middle of the pond with me. At first the glare on the water made it difficult to figure out what it was—a muskrat, a beaver, an otter? It was Molly. She'd come after me.

Molly is what is known as a Nantucket mutt—part yellow lab, part golden retriever, part who knows what. We'd first picked her up from the animal shelter almost seven years ago. Her previous owner had been a carpenter, and her childhood exposure to screaming circular saws and pounding hammers, not to mention the constant stress of trying not to fall off the back of a pickup truck as it careened through the crooked streets of Nantucket, had left Molly an emotional wreck. Despite her flaws, Molly is an extremely loving animal and considers herself a full-fledged member of the family.

Now as I watched her swim toward me, her nose pointed urgently in my direction, it almost seemed as though she'd heard us talking about the River Race and wanted to make sure that we didn't leave her out of our plans. Knowing that Molly must be approaching the end of her endurance, I sailed down to her, rounded up, grabbed her by the collar, and dragged her onto the deck. She was exhausted. As I sailed back toward Melissa and the kids, I patted Molly on the head and told her what a fine and noble dog she was. She lay across the splash rail, trembling affectionately.

Unfortunately, this moment of human-canine bonding was not to last. Melissa stood up and called for Molly, but Molly was not about to budge. So I gave her a push. Shooting a sidelong glance of betrayal at me, she slid over the side and reluctantly swam toward Melissa.

After another forty-five minutes of sailing, I returned to shore. As Melissa, Jennie, and Ethan lay on their beach towels and read in their sunglasses, I unrigged the boat while Molly, who already seemed to have forgiven me, luxuriated on the grass. It was good, it was very good. But something wasn't quite right.

With the advent of spring, the ponds that had given me the sense of security I needed to make it through the grim wilds of fall and winter had begun to feel more and more like a closed system. I now felt the need to try something different, to break out. After my April sail on Sesachacha, only a river would do.

Power in the Pond

On Friday, April 23, Bruce Perry, a friend who was the administrator of the Conservation Commission on Nantucket, called to tell me the town was opening Sesachacha Pond that day. All winter he'd heard me talking about my dream of one day sailing "through the cut." As it turned out, we were scheduled to have dinner with Bruce and his family that night, and since he planned to watch the cut's completion that afternoon, he said he'd tell me about it in the evening.

Bruce and family lived in what's called an upside-down house (bedrooms downstairs, living room and dining room upstairs) overlooking Long Pond in Madaket on the western end of the island. It was the perfect place to hear about a pond opening. Apparently, Sesachacha had been at a record high, so that when they finally completed the cut it had come roaring out in a way that dwarfed the relative trickle I had seen in October. Bruce recounted how fish and even eels were caught up in the rush of water that had quickly carved out an opening the size of a small river. If anything, it should be even bigger by the next afternoon when I planned to go sailing.

"But, Nat," Bruce cautioned, "it's nothing to fool around with. There's an awful lot of power in that pond. And once you're out there in the ocean, you're gone."

That evening, during the drive back into town, I promised Melissa that I was more curious than I was determined to sail through the cut. I just wanted to take a look. And, to be truthful, Bruce's words had had a sobering effect. I wasn't going to go dashing out there like the Lone Ranger. I didn't want to wreck my boat or drown myself. I really didn't.

I spent Saturday morning in the Nantucket Atheneum, the town library. The building, particularly in the wing where the archives were stored, had a Miss Havisham feel to it, as though it were still suspended in a time that the world had long since passed by. Although a spectacular and much-needed renovation project has given the building a whole new ambiance, that morning in the spring of 1993, as I read my way through a stack of ancient letters, I felt as if I too were a kind of artifact blanketed with dust.

By the time I set out for Sesachacha around one o'clock in the afternoon I was anxious to wash off the past and rejoin the present. Melissa, the kids, and Molly were in the car with me. The plan was this: they'd help me with the boat on the southern end of the pond, then drive over to the other side where they'd walk the quarter mile or so to the cut. The subject of my sailing through the cut was studiously avoided.

When we pulled up to the launch ramp, the pond seemed

higher than ever. In the distance we could see the backhoe over on the barrier beach, but from our perspective it looked as though the cut might have closed in overnight—at least that was the claim of an elderly gentleman who'd brought his two dogs for a walk along the pond's edge. "I tell ya," he said, "they should let the old-timers do this kind of thing. These scientific guys don't know what the hell they're doin' when it comes to pond openings."

I was reserving judgment. Appearances, particularly when you're looking at a distant beach, can be deceiving.

The breeze was moderate out of the southwest with plenty of peppy puffs. Soon I was sailing on a beam reach toward where the cut, if there was one, should be. I passed a father and his son fishing in a motorboat. As I entered the midsection of the pond, I saw that Melissa, the kids, and Molly had parked and were now walking along the pond's edge toward the ocean. I waved, but they were too far away to notice.

It was then I realized that there *was* a cut. It was wider than I would ever have imagined—maybe thirty to fifty feet. A virtual torrent of water was rushing through the opening, a white-water river that must have been close to an eighth of a mile long as it curved out toward the sea and collided with the ocean's surf in a distant intermingling of brown and blue waters. I now knew what Bruce had meant when he had spoken of the pond's power, a power that showed no signs of waning more than twenty-four hours after it had first been tapped.

Someone was standing on the northern edge of the pond cut. After watching me for a while, he waved and called out to me. It was Bruce. The question was how to get close enough to speak to him without being immediately sucked out to sea.

I approached cautiously from the north, where a sandbar had been formed by the turbulence at the cut's opening.

"Bruce!" I shouted. "What do you think?"

"Don't do it! The current is really ripping!"

I decided to sail past the pond opening just to give it a look. Although I could feel the current grab my boat, torquing it seaward with a trembling, atavistic lurch, the cut wasn't the all-consuming portal to destruction that I had first assumed it would be. There was enough of a breeze to let me flirt along the opening's edge without losing myself to the current.

The cut was wide. There was plenty of space for me to sail through it, even with my sail all the way out. It also looked fairly deep. I did notice, however, quite a bit of wave action at the end of the cut. In fact, it looked like a sandbar had formed out there. Even if I did make it through the cut alive, how in God's name was I ever going to sail back to the pond? But still the opening beckoned.

Suddenly I was filled with a desire to just close my eyes and surrender myself to the flow. Meanwhile, Melissa and company were gradually making their way along the beach. Should I wait for them? If I did, I might lose my nerve.

I tacked and began to bear away toward the cut.

The Cut

Steep walls of sand loomed on either side, so steep that the sound of rushing water seemed amplified within this friable, curving moat. To my right, lodged within the sand, was the smooth, barkless shape of a tree. To my left I saw Bruce's son Sean standing at the cut's edge watching me.

"Hi, Sean!" I yelled. He looked at me and smiled.

There was a spasmodic, up-and-down motion to the waves, like the rinse cycle of a washing machine, and yet all the time the current was rushing me toward a bare ledge of sand where huge waves from Portugal burst against the pond flow. How was I going to make it across that shoal without getting killed?

It was like a scene in a Fellini movie. Just before I slammed into the sandbar, I saw the figure of the elderly man, hunched over and watching me silently from the left bank. Then I was hurtling into the bar, yanking up my daggerboard and heeling the boat to weather in a desperate attempt to keep from rounding up as the shelving sand nudged my rudder out of the water.

The first wave broke across my deck and swept across the entire boat, nearly filling the cockpit. The force of the wave, and perhaps a back eddy, slowed the boat to the point that I just sat there, hung up on the bar as the ocean ahead coiled into a liquid wall of water. I was a sitting duck.

With my daggerboard and rudder all the way up, I had no steerage, and the next wave spun me around like a top. Now I was sideways to the surf. WHAM! The next wave flipped me over immediately. The water was colder than I had expected and moving very fast. Beginning to panic, I struggled to stay with the boat. I thought for sure the spars had broken like matchsticks against the sand. As the current carried me into deep water, the boat began to turtle—a bad thing to have happen if your daggerboard is all the way up—so I dived underwater and pushed the blade through the trunk.

Climbing up onto the finlike projection of the daggerboard, I glanced toward the rapidly receding shore, a blank, treeless sweep of pale brown sand. Then I looked out toward the wide-open sea, an empty infinity of blue that blended seamlessly with the cloudless sky. A whole new set of fears began to take hold. What if my rig had indeed been damaged? There was no way I was going to paddle my way back to the beach. I was already close to a quarter mile out and going fast.

I righted the boat and was relieved to see that everything was intact. But I had my work cut out for me. Like a furiously deflating balloon, the pond was still blowing me to the east.

I scrambled back onto the boat, slammed the rudder down, yanked in the mainsheet, and started to sail for shore. I could see Melissa and the kids on the beach, waving to me. Bruce and Sean were also there. The old man had disappeared. I was now very aware of the ocean's tidal currents working on the Sunfish, and I still had fears of being pushed out to sea before the eyes of my family.

It was a beat back to the island, and I sailed off on a port tack. The ocean swells had a slow, powerful feel to them, as if I were sailing across the gently heaving breast of a giant beast. It was a lazy, disorienting motion. I tacked and edged over toward the cut, but the water was still wild and dangerous over there so I tacked away, planning my final approach to the beach.

Landing in an ocean swell is not easy. One screwup and a wave can smash the boat into the sand and destroy both the boat and the sailor. In the nineteenth and early twentieth centuries, Nantucket cod fishermen had performed this maneuver in their fish-laden dories on a daily basis, and more than a few of them had been lost on this very same shore.

Soon I was locked on to the face of a big comber. As I teetered on the lip of the giant wave, my mainsail flapping now that the boat was moving faster than the wind, I pulled up my daggerboard and held on for dear life. It was like sitting on a boogie board with a sail on it. The wave took me right up the beach and deposited me with almost delicate precision at the tide line. As the wave retreated, I leapt out, grabbed the bow handle, and pulled my boat beyond the next wave's reach.

Only after my family and Bruce and Sean had joined me did I begin shaking. Bruce had brought a camera with him and had taken some pictures of my voyage through the cut, one of which now hangs in our living room. (If you look carefully you can see the hunched outline of that mysterious old man.) Melissa recounted how they'd watched the top of my sail bouncing up and down as it rushed across the sand and that Molly had run ahead and followed me along the cut. Reluctantly, they agreed to help me lug the boat back to the pond. After only a few rest stops, we made it.

As my support team sat along the cut's edge and watched the water go by, I sailed for another half hour or so. But I was too emotionally drained to do much more than relive what I'd just experienced. What had I been thinking? It had been irresponsible and imprudent, but, wow, what a rush. It occurred to me that I was lucky to be alive.

When it came to pond sailing, I'd reached what the poet Robert Lowell, who'd spent two summers on Nantucket, had called "the end of the whaleroad." I might not have sailed on absolutely every pond the island had to offer, but I'd come as close as I needed to.

If I was going to move forward, to improve, I couldn't do it alone.

PART IV
Down the River

The Nantucketer, he alone resides and riots on the sea; he alone, in Bible language, goes down to it in ships; to and fro ploughing it as his own special plantation. There is his home; there lies his business, which a Noah's flood would not interrupt, though it overwhelmed all the millions in China.

—HERMAN MELVILLE, *Moby-Dick*

Reassembling Childhood

MEMORIAL DAY WEEKEND brought to Nantucket the usual throng of tourists, many of them sailors on racing yachts participating in the annual Figawi Regatta. ("Figawi" comes from the phrase "Where the f— are we?"—a common query when sailing in fog.) Over the last twenty or so years, this race from Hyannis to Nantucket has evolved into a bigger and bigger party. It is also one of the first sure signs that the cold, fogbound state of suspended animation known on Nantucket as spring has given way to the sea breezes of summer.

The Connecticut River Race (officially titled the Lions Club River Classic) was scheduled for the Saturday and Sunday following Memorial Day Weekend. We had reservations on the Thursday noon ferry. Prior to our planned arrival in Hartford on Friday evening, we had more than a dozen errands to run on Cape Cod, from going to the dentist to buying sunscreen and bathing suits. It was to be a typical Philbrick family off-island excursion—three and a half days of frenzy.

Having arranged to pick up one boat at my parents' home in Hyannis, we drove onto the ferry with trailer and one Sunfish in tow. It was a sunny, windy day, and the four of us lingered on the deck for most of the two-and-a-half-hour trip. The view was not only great, but the deck was also the best place to avoid getting seasick. As we approached Hyannis, a swarm of sailboards appeared off the port bow, blasting along in the southwesterly sea breeze and using the ferry's wake to wave-jump as much as ten feet into the air.

After securing my brother's old Sunfish onto the trailer and making sure we had all the right equipment, we spent the night at my parents' house, where Molly the dog would spend the weekend. By two on Friday afternoon we were on our way to Hartford. We were driving across the Bourne Bridge with the Cape Cod Canal stretched out below us when I realized that I had just spent the last two days reassembling my childhood. We had all the elements: two Sunfish (one of which, my brother's, was the first one we'd ever owned), a trailer, and a car with a father, mother, and two kids. And, best of all, we were on our way to a regatta in which all four of us would be sailing.

These days it's very rare that kids and parents race, or even sail, together. The tendency at sailing clubs across the country has been to promote junior classes such as the 420, a two-person racing dinghy, and the Optimist, an eight-foot Frosty-like pram for kids up to fifteen years of age. Since the Optimist is so small, it doesn't intimidate the kids, and as a result they tend to learn much faster. After the kids have competed for five or so years in the Optimist, with their parents driving them hither and yon to regattas, they move into the 420 for three or four more years of junior racing. There is no doubt that this kind of progression provides the kids with a much more thorough and intensive racing background than I ever had. But it robs sailboat racing of one of its most attractive and unique aspects: that of people of all ages competing together.

For me, one of the good things about being a teenager in a sailing family was that it gave the four of us something to talk about. Especially during a long drive to a regatta, my father and I would talk ceaselessly about sailboats. I'd ask him questions not only about the regatta we were going to but about sailing in general, and he would hold forth in his best professorial manner on all things nautical. In contrast to my monochromatic life as a shy, studious kid, sailing was an exotic, endlessly fascinating world, and I drank in every detail. I especially enjoyed my father's tales of what it had been like in his day, when he was racing against future sailing greats like Ted Hood and George O'Day. So as we drove toward Hartford I felt it incumbent upon me to hold forth, if not as a professor, at least as a writer and father. I began a lengthy monologue on the history of the Sunfish class and the River Race, with enlightening digressions on the Philbrick family's singular skill in the naming of boats. By the time we reached Rhode Island, Jennie was nodding, and Ethan was fast asleep.

Logistics

WE PULLED INTO Hartford's Riverside Park a little before 6:00 p.m. This was very much an urban park—a ragged, overgrown place at the edge of the city. It didn't look like a safe spot after dark. But for now, on a warm evening in June, there was an open stillness about it that was reassuring, especially with the Connecticut River flowing beside it, a wide, windless sheet of moving water.

A launch ramp the width of a football field provided ample access. A retired couple in a motorhome with New Jersey plates had arrived before us and had already begun to rig their Sunfish. The husband, a wiry man in a baseball cap, River Race T-shirt, and shorts, told us that this would be their tenth River Race. He added that the park was a good deal safer than it had been a decade ago.

After unloading our boats at the park that evening, we were supposed to drive early the next morning to the race's finish point, Deep River, where we would leave our car and trailer and board a shuttle bus back to Hartford for a

9:00 a.m. start. We unloaded our boats onto the grass, then stuffed our clothes, camping equipment, and food into five different garbage bags, which we then jammed into the boats' cockpits for the night.

The couple from New Jersey assured us that the regatta organizers had arranged for a security guard to watch over the boats, and sure enough, it wasn't long before a polite, uniformed young man drove in, got out of his car, and began to make pleasant small talk as we put the finishing touches on our garbage bags. By seven we were headed south toward Old Saybrook, where we'd booked a motel room for the night.

The drive down Route 9, which roughly paralleled the river, was disturbingly long. With map in hand Melissa ticked off the towns along the way. East Hartford, Glastonbury, Wethersfield, Rocky Hill, Cromwell, Portland, Middletown, Higganum, Haddam, Chester, Selden Neck, and then, finally, Deep River. The drive took an hour and a half! If the winds and the weather weren't in our favor, this could be a very, very long race. At least the current would be with us.

The weather forecast was lousy. Although the day would dawn clear and fresh, clouds and rain were scheduled to move in. Light winds from the southeast were predicted—just the wrong direction. We would have to beat all the way to Hurd State Park, almost thirty miles down the river.

Saturday began with wonderful sun. The dew was glistening and the birds were chirping as we piled into the Cherokee and headed for Deep River Marina, a new, upscale facility with wonderfully clean bathrooms. Regatta organizers told us where to park our cars and trailers, then herded us onto a school bus. Just as we were about to leave, a father and his young daughter dashed onto the bus and we were off. The father looked familiar. For the whole kidney-jolting journey to Hartford, during which Ethan quickly faded off to sleep beside me, I found myself staring at the back of the man's head and racking my brain. Who was this guy?

Once we'd gotten off the bus and I'd had a chance to look him full in the face, I recognized him as Rip Fisher, an old friend from Long Island. Rip's curly blond hair may have been a little thinner, but otherwise he hadn't changed much in the last fifteen years. I first met Rip back in 1973 at the Sunfish North Americans in Newport News, Virginia. I'd been seventeen and there with my brother and my parents; Rip, a few years older and a Dartmouth man, was there with a sailing buddy and two girls. I remember being extremely impressed by not only his sailing ability (he was fast in a blow) but also his casual air of maturity. After greeting Rip and introducing him and his eight-year-old daughter Catherine to the rest of "Team Philbrick," we all began to rig our boats. Our decks were soon heaped with trash bags, held in place with flabby webs of shock cord. The weather was still picture perfect, even if the wind was somewhat light. Maybe, just maybe, the weatherman had it all wrong.

Melissa was going to be racing with the old, smaller sail that came with my brother's boat. I'd offered to buy her a new one, but she'd insisted on staying with Sam's original equipment. "It'll give me an excuse," she explained. When most of the sails in the twenty-nine-boat fleet had been raised, it became clear that she was not going to be alone.

Roughly half the fleet was still in the dark ages when it came to sails; this was a group in which boat speed was not an especially high priority. Still, I could see that there were a half dozen state-of-the-art boats, including Rip's. But wasn't it kind of ridiculous to think about going fast when you were sharing deck space with garbage bags? Old habits die hard.

After a brief skippers' meeting at the launch ramp, during which it was explained that our voyage was to be divided into a total of five races (three on the first day, two on the second), it was time to head onto the river. Ethan and I shoehorned ourselves into the cockpit and ventured into the current. The water was certainly moving, but in an entirely different way from the Sesachacha cut. Instead of rushing, this water was sliding with a powerful dignity that seemed unimaginably old.

Soon we were in danger of being swept under the bridge, so Ethan and I beat a hasty retreat back to shore. The couple we'd met the evening before were already over there, hanging on to the branch of a tree. This looked like a good strategy, but available branches were hard to come by. It was then that the tip of our spar got hung up in the trees overhead. Although this kept us from being swept down the river, it was not an especially good thing for our sail, which seemed dangerously close to ripping as the water sped past and the tips of the branches poked into the sail.

"Goddammit," I muttered as I tried to scull us out of the trees.

"What's wrong?" Ethan asked.

"Oh, nothing."

"We're stuck in this tree, aren't we, Dad?"

"Well, yeah."

I was feeling inept and flustered in a race that was supposed to be carefree and fun. If ever there was a Ferdinand the Bull race, this was it. But no, here I was, tangled up in a tree and cursing. As I flailed away, green leaves raining down on the deck, I noticed that Melissa and Jennie, along with Rip and Catherine, were playing it cool and hanging out at the dock beside the launch ramp. Of course, this only made me feel all the more inept and flustered.

Meanwhile, the race committee—two guys in an aluminum fishing boat with a small outboard—was setting up a starting line just upstream of the bridge. After one last flurry of leaves, Ethan and I finally disentangled ourselves from the tree and began to make our way toward the starting line. "BEEP!"

True to form, the race committee had just given us a surprise start, and we were still a good half minute from the line. A handful of boats were poised to take advantage of the race committee's spontaneity, while the rest of us crossed the line in our own good time.

The Connecticut River Race had officially begun.

Rollin'

We were underneath the bridge, the sail strapped in, with Ethan down to leeward and me squatting in the cockpit. Ethan looked up into the girdered, pigeon-infested complexity of the bridge. It was cool and dark, with a faintly metallic scent in the air.

"Think there's an echo?" Ethan asked.

"Give it a try."

"Yo!"

Melissa and Jennie were just a little way behind us. "Yo!" answered Jennie. We all agreed that, yes, indeed, there was an echo.

Meanwhile the wind, which had been extremely unsettled as we drifted underneath the bridge, settled down a bit. We had a direct beat to windward, with factories and warehouses on either side of the river, which now seemed to have changed, chameleon-like, from blue to a gritty, industrial gray. I tacked on a wind shift. Half a minute later, I tacked again. I asked Ethan how we were doing.

"We're beating Mommy and Jennie."

Despite their old-style sail, they were doing surprisingly well. I pointed toward Rip and Catherine, who were right on our heels, and told Ethan to keep an eye on them. He watched them like a hawk.

We found ourselves tacking at regular intervals. With all the garbage bags and with Ethan aboard, the boat was certainly heavier than I was used to. Indeed, *Rosebud* had an almost keelboat-ish momentum to it as we ghosted through the lulls and searched out the puffs, the wakes of passing motorboats slapping hollowly against the hull.

Rosebud. I had used my boat's long-lost name. My children had rolled their eyes when I revealed the name I had given my boat after watching *Citizen Kane* in college. Given yesterday's revelation, it now seemed only appropriate to call my Sunfish by name. Suddenly the boat seemed less like a disposable Bic shaver and more like a member of the family. *Rosebud.* With all of our belongings aboard and Ethan with me in the cockpit and Melissa and Jennie not far behind in *Poisson* (my brother Sam's boat), these were no longer single-handed racing dinghies; these were Arks on which we sailed, two by two.

As we tacked our way around the first bend in the river, I noticed that Rip and Catherine were not the only team we had to worry about. There was another mixed doubles team that looked very sharp. Ethan thought their boat was cool because it had so many stickers on it. The one on their transom read FOLLOW ME, I KNOW WHERE I'M GOING. I asked Ethan if we should do what it said. He shook his head.

Although Ethan had demonstrated enormous powers of concentration for the first half hour of the race, routinely informing me of where the "sticker boat" and "Rip" and "Mommy and Jennie" were, the novelty soon began to wear off.

Ethan, a seven-year-old recorder and flute player, has always been a very musical child. He had learned how to read music before he learned how to read words. So, with the garbage-bag shock cords providing a basslike accompaniment, we sang songs—some of them old favorites ("Baby Beluga"), some of them of our own devising. Ethan would sing the melody; I'd harmonize as best I could. At one point we attempted a Connecticut River version of the song that made Ike and Tina Turner famous:

> *Left my good wife with my daughter*
> *In an ol' boat, she barely does float,*
> *But I just had to leave her—*
> *'Cause we're rollin' . . . (Rollin'!)*
> *Rollin' down da riva.*

> *The wind is too light for sailin',*
> *If it rains we'll soon be bailin',*
> *The weathergirl I don't believe her—*
> *'Cause we're rollin' . . . (Rollin'!)*
> *Rollin' down da riva . . .*

We had other lyrics, but neither Ethan nor I could remember them the next morning.

We'd been racing for a little more than an hour. If anything, there was less wind than when we'd started. By maintaining our aggressive, quick-tack strategy we'd worked out a sizable lead. In the meantime Ethan and I kept singing as the riverscape gradually shifted from industrial to rural. Instead of factories and warehouses, there were fields and forests as the river shifted from a uniform gray to a swirling mix of blues and browns. Unfortunately, clouds had begun to appear above the western shore.

Up ahead I spotted the committee boat and a buoy. Our first race was apparently coming to an end. As we finished, the race committee directed us toward a tree-shaded, slate-colored beach on the eastern shore. The second we touched land, Ethan and I headed into the woods to take advantage of our few moments of privacy. Almost immediately we were swallowed up by what seemed like an almost primeval forest of towering trees, thick vines, and waist-deep ferns. It was so wild and lush that I felt as though I were choking on chlorophyll. And we were only a few miles downriver from the biggest city in Connecticut.

By the time we emerged from the forest, the rest of the fleet had begun to arrive. In a pattern that would persist throughout the weekend, the race committee assigned finishes to those in the back of the fleet and towed the stragglers to the finish.

Melissa and Jennie had finished a highly respectable fifth overall in the race, the first boat with an old sail. Rip and Catherine had finished third, and it wasn't long before we met Malcolm Dickinson and Sarah Harms, the team on board the "sticker boat." Malcolm was a recent graduate of

Yale; Sarah was soon to graduate. I'd heard about Malcolm from my parents. Originally from Chicago, he'd been a fixture on the Sunfish circuit during the last couple of years and had developed a reputation as a solid light-air sailor. In May he'd won the annual Bolton Lake Regatta, a one-day event that traditionally attracts New England's top Sunfish sailors. To know that Malcolm had done so well at that regatta made our first race win all the more rewarding.

We didn't have long to gab on the beach. Since the wind was light and from the wrong direction, we were already way behind schedule if we were going to reach Hurd State Park before nightfall. Almost as soon as the last boat was towed to the finish, the committee was once again performing one of its off-the-cuff starts.

As it turned out, one boat was positioned to make the most of it. Ethan and I referred to it as the "Party Boat." These guys were true Connecticut River pros. They had a beer cooler that was the perfect size for a Sunfish cockpit. They had a radio that hung off the boom. Since there was no place for them in the cockpit, they reclined on the aft and forward decks, with cushions to keep them comfortable. They sipped mixed drinks from foam-insulated sport cups and were having one helluva good time, and for two and a half minutes they were leading.

Once again, Ethan and I worked out into the lead, with Rip and Catherine and Malcolm and Sarah behind us. The weather was deteriorating dramatically. As the clouds moved in, the temperature dropped; rain now looked like an inevitability.

The river began to curve quite a bit, but no matter how much it curved, the wind always seemed to be right on our noses. Given that we were sailing a serpentine course, the river naturally divided itself into separate sections, where entirely different sets of wind shifts prevailed. This meant that once the fleet sorted itself out soon after the start, the gap between boats began to increase, until by an hour or so into the race, the distances between boats was, relatively speaking, huge.

From my perspective it was great. With the river curving this way and that, it didn't take long before we were enjoying puffs and slants of wind that the boats behind us never even saw. In fact, Ethan complained about how boring it was since there weren't any other boats near us. For me, it was a most splendid isolation, our wake extending out in a gradually widening V that seemed to reach out beyond the shores of this river to the invisible edges of the universe itself.

Maybe, just maybe, all those months on Nantucket's ponds and that long weekend in Florida were beginning to pay off. But then I began to wonder: What possible relevance could a two-person race with garbage bags on deck have to racing in the Sunfish North Americans? For now, at least, I wasn't going to let it worry me.

A man in a motorboat began to finish us on a rolling basis. This was the race organizer, Dick Campbell, a buoyant "let's go for it" kind of guy in an Australian bush-style hat, who pointed at us and shouted, "The winner!" and took off toward the rest of the fleet. Ethan urged me to turn back so we could search out Melissa and Jennie. Not long after

we'd found them (they'd finished seventh), the race committee decided it was time for a collective tow.

Part of the equipment required for the River Race is a
twenty-foot towline, and during that first day it was a line
with which Ethan and I became highly familiar. Our particular string of boats included twelve Sunfish, of which our
two were the last. Ahead of us were two guys with a little
yellow rubber ducky with dark sunglasses suspended from
the upper spar. It wasn't until our tow had ended at Rocky
Hill, a small section of dirty brown beach on the western
shore, that we learned that the ducky was the race's perpetual trophy. The previous year's winner is required to "display" the ducky throughout the following year's race.

On the beach we ate lunch and got to know Mark and
Max Weiner, the winners of this fabled rubber ducky. They
were a father and son who had driven all the way from
Rochester, New York. As it turned out, Mark had also attended the Midwinters, and once he'd taken off the hood of
his raingear I recognized him as one of the sailors who had
been fighting it out in the trenches with me.

Rocky Hill was a place of three-wheeled recreational ve-
hicles; there was also a huge RV out of which emerged one
of the crew members of the "Party Boat" in a full-length wet
suit and, of course, a drink in hand.

By now it was raining fairly steadily. The temperature
had plunged into the sixties and was still falling. Ethan and
I were both in foul weather gear and doing occasional jumping jacks to keep the blood flowing. Then, miraculously, a

breeze from the north sprang up, giving us a run down the river. Soon Dick Campbell was dashing around the beach like a madman.

At first I wasn't sure what he was up to, then I realized that we were in the midst of a Le Mans–style start. When Dick pointed at your boat and said, "You—go!" that's exactly what you were supposed to do.

So as Dick approached, Ethan and I readied our boat for what was to be the final race of the day, and, shouting some encouraging words to Melissa and Jennie, we pushed good ole *Rosebud* into the river.

The Deluge

THE WIND GODS had been only toying with us. Less than ten minutes into the third race, the breeze had died and shifted back into the south. Then it started to rain.

The word "rain" does not do justice to the level of precipitation we encountered. It pounded on our heads and backs. It flowed down the sails, pooled along the boom, then dumped on us like an upturned bucket when we tacked. The sponge in our cockpit began to float. We lost all hope of having a warm dry tent that night. We knew our sleeping bags were probably soaked. And still the members of Team Philbrick pushed on heroically. We tacked. We adjusted our sails. We watched the competition. We froze.

The river meandered and so did we, sailing so slowly across its rain-pelted surface that this final race of the day seemed like it would never end. Finally, at 4:30, Dick Campbell appeared in his motorboat and once again declared us the winner. The only other boat in sight was the sticker-covered one crewed by Malcolm and Sarah.

Instead of turning back and looking for Mommy and Jennie, Ethan wanted to keep going. By this point he was so cold and bored that the thought of backtracking was more than he could bear. I agreed. While Dick and his compatriots in their smaller boats collected the rest of the fleet, Ethan and I, along with Malcolm and Sarah, were given a tow by the flagship of the River Race, a classic wooden motorboat of close to thirty feet that just happened to be in our vicinity when the race ended.

Even though the rain was still coming down and the afternoon was already looking like evening, Ethan and I were in pretty good spirits, assuming that Hurd State Park must be just around the bend. We began by telling each other jokes.

"Why do cows wear bells?"

"In case their horns don't work."

"What did the cannibal say to the sleeping missionary?"

"Ah, breakfast in bed."

An hour later, the jokes were getting pretty stale and the rain was still coming down. Nothing that even vaguely resembled a campground was anywhere in sight. The only excitement was watching Malcolm and Sarah cuddle underneath their Sunfish sail. Finally, after sitting in the two inches of water at the bottom of the cockpit without saying anything for five or ten minutes, Ethan turned to me and said, "Dad."

"Yeah?"

"You know what?"

"What."

"This sucks."

"Ethan."

"Yeah?"

"You're right."

By now it was approaching six in the evening, and I was worried that Ethan was becoming hypothermic. I asked the couple who were running the motor yacht if he might be able to stay with them inside their cabin. That Ethan readily agreed to go on board indicated just how miserable he was feeling.

As we made the transfer I asked how far we had to go. The man winced. "At least an hour, I'm afraid."

They treated Ethan like a prince. They took off his wet socks, put on dry ones, and wrapped him in a blanket. They also gave him something to eat. Ten minutes later he'd fallen asleep.

Meanwhile, I watched the river go by. If the weather hadn't been so bad, this would have been an absolute delight. There were fascinating houses built on tree-covered cliffs and on levee-like banks that must have flooded on a fairly regular basis. But there was more to the river than just scenery.

Ever since the Dutch explorer Adriaen Block sailed up it in 1614, the Connecticut River has played an important part in the economic development of southern New England. In the seventeenth century, Indian-supplied beaver pelts found their way down the river to coastal trading posts. By the nineteenth century, the river itself was powering machine tool and small arms factories in Hartford, Middletown, and other river towns. Today a nuclear power plant in Haddam relies on the Connecticut's waters to cool its core. Yet despite the commercial uses, it was obvious on that cold, wet evening in June that the Connecticut River still possessed a wild beauty that not even the yellowing and pitted dome of the Connecticut Yankee Power Plant could upstage.

Sometime after 7:00 p.m. Hurd State Park came into view over on the eastern bank—a grassy clearing fronted by a breakwater of large brown rocks and backed by a hillside whose towering trees cast the campsite in a dank gloom. As the four of us set up our two tents, Melissa and Jennie recounted how they had been so cold and so bored during the two-and-a-half-hour tow that they had come up with a way of playing Stone, Paper, Scissors using a combination of head signals and facial expressions. This enabled them to keep their wet, frozen hands in their pockets. Melissa ultimately lost to Jennie, 49 to 50.

Even before we had our tents up, it began to rain again. Although the Lions Club had put together a spectacular spread, it was difficult to demonstrate much enthusiasm as the rain drummed on the tarps overhead. In the interests of reducing their baggage, Rip and Catherine had elected not to bring a tent and planned to sleep underneath their outstretched sail, not a fun prospect in this much rain.

What made the miserable conditions worse was the thought of how much fun the race could have been in decent weather. We heard tales of the campfires and sing-alongs of previous years and stared moodily into the wet darkness. Before he and Catherine entered their sleeping bags for a soggy night's sleep, Rip and I talked a little bit. He was working for Goldman Sachs; his territory was Canada. He now had three children and his plan was to give each one of them a chance to sail in the River Race.

At nine we decided to turn in—Ethan and Jennie in one tent, Melissa and I in the other. We were all exhausted and cold and a sleeping bag was our only hope of keeping warm.

As I lay there on the cold wet ground in my cold wet sleeping bag with a busted zipper and listened to the rain pound on the tent roof, I asked myself the inevitable question: Why? Why in a world of Jacuzzis and central heating were we submitting ourselves and our children to this kind of discomfort, all in the name of sport?

Melissa adjusted the bag of clothes that served as her pillow.

"I guess this wasn't such a good idea," I said.

"What do you mean?"

"This weather—what could be worse?"

"But the kids are having a good time."

"Think so?"

"You should have heard Ethan bragging to his sister about winning three races."

"How about Jennie, what's she think?"

Melissa reached for my hand and squeezed it. "We're having fun," she assured me before drifting off to sleep.

Sail to the Sea

At 6:10 A.M., I woke to hear Jennie and Ethan talking next door, their words indecipherable above the thrumming of raindrops on our tents. After rising, we had a breakfast to end all breakfasts served beneath the tarps. Then we had to pack up all our wet stuff into garbage bags, and, yes, the rain continued. But there was hope. The wind, although light, was now out of the north. The forecast was for sun in the afternoon. Things could only improve.

The wretched weather had taken its toll. Soon after yet another surprise start, we found ourselves beside a father-and-son team in the midst of a fight. The teenage son apparently had little faith in his father's tactical judgment. They were bickering about which jibe they should be on when the father finally erupted: "Look, I've had it up to here with all this male bonding bullshit. Will you please SHUT UP?" Ethan and I couldn't help but snicker, even though I realized that in ten years we might very well be in the same position.

If yesterday's racing had at times felt like a slow crawl up a cliff, now it seemed as if we had reached the summit and were finally sliding down the mountain—our sails out and the wind hastening us along in ever strengthening gusts. The river was also changing, widening until it contained some quite sizable islands. At one point we reached a crisis. There was an island up ahead, and for the life of us, Ethan and I couldn't figure out which way to go: Should we leave the island to port or starboard? As it turned out, half the fleet went one way, the other half went the other way. After about twenty minutes of nail biting, it became clear that it hadn't made much difference either way.

Gradually, ever so gradually, the breeze began to build and the rain began to lessen until it was blowing close to fifteen knots and the sun was peeking through the clouds. Initially, Malcolm and Sarah were out in front, but soon it was a virtual dead heat with them and us and Rip and Catherine sailing side by side. The proximity of the competition and the building wind made it an extremely exciting race. Ethan was my play-by-play man.

"Dad, we're catching the sticker boat. We've got their wind!"

"Think so?"

"Look!"

"But how about Rip and Catherine, don't they have ours?"

"Maybe . . ."

After about a half hour of trading places back and forth, we'd worked our way into a marginal lead. It was then, in full view of the fleet, that Ethan was hit with an overpowering urge to urinate. Experience had long since taught us that when Ethan has to pee, Ethan has to pee. Unfortunately, we were in the midst of a fight for first, and worst of all, Ethan had his lifejacket and wet suit on.

But not to worry. The lifejacket came off in a flash. The shorty-style wet suit was not so easy, however. I pulled down the back zipper and then, standing on the aft deck, with his legs straddling the tiller, Ethan frantically pulled down the suit and let her fly to leeward.

"Hey!" Rip shouted. "What's going on up there?" If Ethan was mortified, he didn't show it. Soon he'd put himself back together and we were crossing the finish line with another first. We slapped each other five.

The race committee directed us to a nearby sandbar where the fleet assembled before the start of our final leg. A whole different attitude prevailed. People were smiling; we were almost home.

For the final start, the committee gave us a traditional three-minute sequence. Soon we were once again neck and neck with Rip and Catherine and Malcolm and Sarah, and once again we were able to establish a narrow lead. The cool northerly breeze scrubbed away the clouds and roughed up the water into a white-flecked craze of blue silver. Even the shoreline seemed transformed by the freshening wind, the once rolling hills giving way to craggy cliffs, where majestic houses shared space with soaring eagles. By the time we passed the incongruous medieval bulk of Gillette Castle in Hadlyme, the gusts were up to twenty knots. The wind was shifting back and forth as much as 30 degrees, requiring that we jibe frequently if we were to use the shifts to our tactical advantage.

Jibing a Sunfish with two people and garbage bags on the deck is not easy. It's difficult to position both people so that the mainsheet doesn't catch one of them when the sail comes across. Although we eventually worked out a system, our first heavy-air jibe caught Ethan's fingers in the mainsheet. With two boats breathing down our necks, I had little attention left for the crew, and Ethan seemed fine.

Ever since the kids were very young, I've been telling them the story of the Spartan boy who, rather than admit that he had a fox hidden underneath his shirt, allowed the animal to savagely attack him. The Spartan boy was so stoically tough that he didn't let out a single peep as the fox gnawed out his vitals. It wasn't until the Spartan boy fell over dead that anyone had any idea of what was going on. So whenever my kids get hurt, they can count on me to mention the Spartan boy, an admittedly insensitive and maybe even cruel stratagem to put their pain in perspective.

It took a few moments after we had finished our jibe for me to realize that Ethan had been hurt. He was clutching his finger and muttering to himself. At first I couldn't figure out what it was he was saying, and then I heard him. He was saying "Spartan boy" over and over again, trying to fight back tears. Suddenly I was overwhelmed by my own responsibility in placing my seven-year-old son in such a demanding and intense situation. The unexpected fortitude he was displaying undid me. I wanted to weep with him.

Ethan ultimately shook off the pain, and we increased

our lead until we were by ourselves and not sure of where we were going. By this stage, the river had widened to the extent that it looked less like a flowing river and more like a tidal, inland sea. On the western shore we saw a group of moored boats, one of which was a Beetle Cat that could have been a dead ringer for the one we had back home on Nantucket. After two days of sailing down a river, we were back on familiar territory.

Eventually Dick Campbell caught up with us in his motorboat and directed us toward a giant stone piling near the western shore where a man was standing with a clipboard. A half hour later we were back at the Deep River Marina for another great spread of food and an awards ceremony. Melissa and Jennie had finished fifth overall and third in the Odd Couple division. Ethan and I had finished first in both our division and overall, earning us the Rubber Ducky. Best of all, though, was that Ethan won the Youngest Participant Award.

During the drive back to Hyannis, I thought about the last two days of sailing. I now realized that the Zone—at least the "old" Zone—had so far eluded me. Although I had had my moments, the sense of cosmic connection I had felt was more on the order of sniffing the flowers instead of goring the matador, which, given the context of this regatta, was just as well. It was Ethan I found myself thinking about as we drove up I-95.

Inevitably, I began to compare our relationship on the water to how it had been between my father and me. Even though sailing was common to both relationships, I marveled at how different it was for Ethan. When it came to sailing, my father had always stayed in the background. Even though the sport had been central to his own youth, he had never thrust it upon my brother and me. He let us discover it on our terms. Only after I had begged and pleaded for a Sunfish did he buy us one; only after Sam and I had established ourselves as Sunfish racers had he bought one for himself. He had given us space.

At times, I remember, it had seemed like too much space. When I qualified at sixteen for the Sunfish Worlds in Martinique, my parents had said, yes, I could go, but I'd have to do it without them. So Sam, who was fourteen, and I (the youngest participant in the regatta) went by ourselves. A Caribbean resort proved a bit much for the two of us. While most of my competitors partied late into the night, Sam and I spent our evenings holed up in our room in numb seclusion.

Looking back, I wondered whether I was now overcompensating for my parents' shadowy presence along the peripheries of my sailing life. Poor Ethan and Jennie. Every weekend dedicated to yet another episode in the miniseries *Daddy Sails the Ponds*. I could see now that I was making it difficult for them to take up sailing with the passion and persistence that had ruled my adolescence. They would, most probably, search out other avenues. For now, Ethan had his flute and Jennie had her swimming. I only hoped that I hadn't robbed them of something they might have found precious.

But you never know. Later that night, after we'd taken the late boat back to Nantucket and Ethan had fallen asleep, at last in his own bed, the trophy was still in his hands.

Part V
Showtime

We are like the whalers who have been on a long chase. We have at last got the harpoon into the monster, but we must now look how we steer, or with one flop of his tail he will send us all into eternity.

—ABRAHAM LINCOLN

In Limbo

THE SUNDAY OF FOURTH of July weekend found Team Philbrick on Coatue, the sand spit on the northern edge of Nantucket Harbor. In the four weeks since the River Race, I had sailed my Sunfish only twice. My duties at the Nantucket Yacht Club had resumed, making it all but impossible to find time for my own sailing. I'd make plans to practice and then something would always seem to come up. Here I was, showing promise with a month to go but unable to find the sailing time when it really counted. By Fourth of July weekend I had resigned myself to whatever the future held. Since I had less than a week before the North Americans, I told myself that I might as well relax; it was too late to do much of anything else.

Adding to this sense of ineluctable fate was the appearance of Marc, the same old friend who had witnessed the beginning of my training program back on Columbus Day. With Marc's arrival, a circle (perhaps a little lopsided and with a few wobbles in it) had been turned, and it was only right that we all go for a sail. So on a cloudless, almost wind-less Sunday afternoon, we headed for one of the scalloped beaches on the harbor side of Coatue. Jennie sailed with me on old *Rosebud*, while Melissa, Ethan, and Marc delivered the cooler and beach towels in the Beetle Cat.

After throwing out the Beetle's anchor and pulling the Sun-fish onto the beach, we broke out the sandwiches. We soon discovered that we were surrounded by nesting gulls, some of whose eggs had already hatched. At one point a mother and her three downy babies ambled down to the water's edge, then paddled out and back like a family of ducks.

Taking my cue from the gulls, I cajoled Jennie into making her first solo in the Beetle Cat while I sailed the Sunfish. We headed for two buoys that mark the harbor channel running beside the Coatue shore. The breeze was perfect for Jennie; it was also perfect for my last sail before the North Americans since these were, in all likelihood, just the kind of conditions I would encounter in Springfield.

It worked out to be a beat up to one buoy, then a run down to the other. With almost no help from me, Jennie tacked and jibed her way around our little course as I sailed circles around her, using the Beetle as a kind of moving tar-get. Jennie talked the whole time, commenting on the fact that my bathing suit was revealing far too much of my back-side ("Dad, you're mooning me!"), daring me to go swim-ming amid the red jellyfish floating past us, and finally throwing a bailer full of bilgewater in my direction. It was a wonderful sail.

But by the time we returned to the beach, a sudden and

unexpected lassitude had taken over me. After pulling up the Sunfish, I collapsed onto a blanket and felt myself almost immediately drifting toward sleep.

Melissa went out in the Sunfish. Marc, also soloing for the first time in his life, took out the Beetle. As Jennie and Ethan swam, I lay there on my blanket, my eyes almost precisely at water level. Sailboats lurched across water chopped up by Jet Skis and motorboats. With my preparation (such as it was) behind me, and with less than a week until the North Americans in Springfield, I lay there, adrift in a limbo of waiting, and faded off to sleep.

Taking Measure

THE WEATHER NEWS during the week before my departure was all about the terrible flooding of the Mississippi. My arrival in St. Louis confirmed the worst: everywhere there were broken levees, marooned farms, whole towns abandoned to T. S. Eliot's "brown god" and its murky, inexorable waters. As I drove across the empty reaches of southern Illinois I found myself nervously checking the rearview mirror, half expecting to see a cresting tidal wave pursuing me across the hot prairie.

By the time I checked into my motel room in Springfield, it had begun to rain. After calling Melissa and the kids, I lay back on the bed and listened. First there was the rumble of distant thunder, then a light drumming on the thin flat roof that gradually built into a roar. Curious, I ventured out into the hallway and watched through a window. Tree branches were whipping hysterically as the rain came down in jagged, savage sheets. An hour later and all was quiet once again, the puddles on the warm parking lot sending up wispy clouds of steam.

At eight o'clock the next morning I arrived at the Island Bay Yacht Club on Lake Springfield. The air-conditioned clubhouse, built into the side of a grassy hill overlooking the lake, had the dark, big-timbered feel of a ski lodge. Photographs of commodores past and present lined the front hall. One of them was the father of regatta cochairman Todd Gay, whom I'd met at the Midwinters in March. There was definitely a family resemblance.

Since Todd had not yet arrived, and he and he alone knew the location of my borrowed boat, I decided to take an exploratory walk around the premises. Boats were everywhere, either on trailers in the parking lot or scattered across the yacht club grass. But if there were plenty of boats, there were not yet many people; it was still early.

One boat, however, was being carefully scrutinized by its owner. He had his sail up, and he was studying it. I smiled. It was Jeff Linton from Sarasota, the same guy who had helped me rig my boat the night before the Midwinters.

In Sarasota Jeff had been the laid-back local ace. Tall and slender, with a mustache and long curly hair that hung down from the back of his baseball cap, he had reminded me of Robin Hood in the animated Disney movie: an affable, long-necked fox. On the racecourse Jeff had been a notch below the front-runners, ultimately finishing fifth while his training partner Rod Koch, the defending North American champ, had come on strong in the final two races to finish second overall. Jeff had struck me as an excellent sailor who had not yet found the knockout punch of a champion.

But now, as he shook my hand and motioned toward the

windless lake and smiled, Jeff was a changed man. He exuded an intangible quality of confidence, a focused intensity that hadn't been there in Florida. He explained that he'd already been in Springfield for a couple of days to practice. Indeed, he seemed more at ease at this regatta site than he had during the Midwinters in his own backyard; it almost seemed as if the Island Bay Yacht Club were already his domain.

Later I would learn that in the months since the Midwinters, Jeff had made the leap to another level. Rather than being the perpetual bridesmaid to Rod, he had begun to beat him on a regular basis. Instead of an also-ran, Jeff came to Springfield with the expectation of becoming a champion, and you could see it in his eyes. Jeff Linton had entered the Zone.

Once back at the club I was finally able to track down Todd Gay, who was Springfield's local ace. It quickly became clear that Todd was so consumed with the myriad details of organizing the event that all the advantages of being on his home turf had been, for the time being at least, lost to him. Having run more than a few events myself, I knew what he was going through.

In between distractions, Todd directed me to my boat. It wasn't far from Jeff's, and it lay there on the grass with the forlorn air of an orphan: dirty, sailless, and with a vague arc gouged into the forward deck by the spars. A lump came to my throat. This Sunfish, sporting a faded red-white-and-blue racing stripe, looked almost exactly like old *Rosebud* back on Nantucket.

Although the hull seemed in pretty good shape, there were a few scratches that needed some attention. During the next few hours I filled in the gouges with epoxy and sanded them down. Even if it would never be as perfect as the nearly new hull I'd sailed at the Midwinters, this Sunfish, complete with age spots and wrinkles, already felt like an old and trustworthy friend.

Besides filling and sanding the hull, I also needed to install some hardware. But what I needed more than anything else, as the sun climbed in the sky, was some shade. A few extra tools wouldn't have hurt, either.

Enter Joel Furman, an attorney and past North American champ who was the official class measurer for the regatta. As measurer, Joel was required to inspect every boat at the regatta, a daylong process that the heat would turn into an agonizing ordeal. Joel, however, had come prepared. He'd parked his huge station wagon crammed with tools under a tree on the crest of the hill. He'd also brought along a sombrero the diameter of a hula hoop. Most important, he'd brought along his sense of humor, which meant that he was able to take the inevitable static he encountered ("Whaddaya mean my daggerboard's too big?") in stride.

Joel had been at the Midwinters, where he and I had had a similar, almost identical, experience on the race course. Seeing him now, it was as though we were taking up exactly where we'd left off in Florida—on the lawn with our boats. Offering me not only the use of his tools but the shade of his tree, he set out in search of boats to measure.

As I worked away at *Rosebud II*, Joel would check in every

now and then to get a drink and shoot the breeze. By three o'clock, the heat was really beginning to get to him. He sat on his tailgate, sipping water and wiping the sweat from his forehead.

"The hell with this," he said.

"You must be dying," I said. "This heat is unbelievable."

"You know, I'd much rather be back in my air-conditioned law office than wasting my vacation time here. I'm not gonna spend the whole week sitting on a Sunfish and sweating. I'm going home tomorrow. The hell with it."

"What?"

"You heard me. When I'm done measuring, I'm out of here."

As it turned out, Joel ended up staying for the duration of the regatta, which from my perspective made all the difference. Because when things began to turn bad in the days ahead, it would be a few simple words of advice from Joel that would save me from myself.

Doppelgänger

THAT EVENING THERE was a welcoming buffet and skippers' meeting, and as I waited in line for my food, I surveyed the crowd. There were a lot of familiar faces. Besides Jeff, Todd, and Joel, there was Malcolm Dickinson from the River Race. Although last year's champ, Rod Koch, had not yet arrived, Bob Findlay, the current Midwinter champ, was here, as were the Cliftons—the family from Sarasota who had organized the Midwinters—and Eduardo Cordero, a young Venezuelan sailing instructor who had finished an impressive fourth in Florida.

Sitting quietly beside talkative Bob Findlay was Donnie Martinborough from the Bahamas, a tall, deeply tanned man in his mid-thirties with curly blond hair and a colorful button-down shirt. Since I'd last seen him in 1978, he'd won the Sunfish Worlds a total of three times. This was clearly a man to be reckoned with.

I was putting food on my plate and beginning to feel some of the same sense of dislocation I'd known at the Midwinters when someone tapped me on the shoulder. I turned and saw a guy who was a few inches shorter than me, thin, and with a baseball cap on backward.

"Hi, Nat," he said, his voice breaking into an embarrassed laugh. My God, it was Paul Fendler.

If there'd been one person against whom I had always measured myself on the racecourse, it had been Paul Fendler. We had both started racing Sunfish in the early seventies. I'd traveled with my brother and our parents; Paul had traveled with his father. At our first North Americans in Devils Lake, Michigan (which, I now realized, bore an eerie resemblance to Lake Springfield), I had finished twelfth and Paul eleventh, qualifying both of us for the Worlds that winter in Martinique.

That had been in 1972, when we were both sixteen, and over the next six or so years Paul and I had maintained an ongoing rivalry. While Paul had won the Worlds in Venezuela, I had won the North Americans in Barrington, where Paul had finished third; then, the following summer we'd both competed at the Worlds in Medemblik, Holland (the last major regatta for both of us, it turned out), with Paul finishing third to my fourth.

When it came to sailboat racing, Paul and I were wired in very much the same way. We both took it seriously, more seriously than either one of us would have cared to admit, and as a consequence we never became close friends. We were civil to each other, but I couldn't think of any one time when the two of us had taken the opportunity to just hang out and talk. There was always an unstated element of tension between us, and any attempt to delve beneath the surface would have been doomed to failure. The truth of the matter was, of course, we were too much alike: a pair of doppelgängers who shared a single, overweening ambition.

That evening, for the first time in twenty-two years, Paul and I hung out and talked. Almost immediately we hit it off. While being a writer, at-home parent, and sailing director had kept me from fitting comfortably into a traditional career path, Paul was a CPA who worked part time out of his house, with time to do a variety of unusual things: perform in musicals, train for marathons, and read voraciously. Both of us, we decided, were destined to become late bloomers.

Inevitably we began to talk about the old days, referring to our prior competitive personas with a mixture of awe and horror. We both agreed that our dedication to Sunfish racing had been something of a mixed blessing. While it had given us a focus and direction during what is, for almost everyone, a fairly unfocused time, sailing had also limited our exposure to life. Even when we traveled to a world championship in a foreign country, we had rarely seen much of anything beyond the regatta site. For a competitive small boat sailor, the race course is all.

My question was this: If Sunfish racing had indeed provided us with a kind of safe haven from the terrors of the real world, had it been a haven that helped to prepare us in any way for that world? Paul initially seemed to have his doubts, then said, "But you know, Nat, there are things that sailing did teach me—emotional things, about my relationship with other people." Paul laughed. "And a lot of it was, I hate to admit, negative. That's why I had to stop sailing. I realized I was taking it too seriously. I wasn't having fun anymore. It was time I moved on."

But what had we moved on to? For my younger brother Sam, the Sunfish had come to represent all those youthful experiences you have to leave behind in order to grow up. Now a banker and a golfer, Sam had not only given me his old Sunfish, he'd even bought a cruising boat with a head (boatspeak for a bathroom) on it. When he'd heard I was giving the Sunfish another try, he'd sighed and said, "Good for you, Nat." The implication was clear: Would I ever grow up?

Sam had a point. If the sole reason I'd begun this come-back was to prove that I still wasn't too old, it was going to be an exercise in futility. But maybe by compartmentaliz-ing his life into childhood and adulthood experiences, Sam was running the risk of cheating himself. But out of what, exactly? I hoped I'd have a better idea by the end of the regatta.

In the meantime I had another question for Paul. Why, after all these years, had we both ended up here in Spring-field, Illinois? Paul had a theory: "They say it takes seven years for the body to completely replace all its cells. I think with every cycle you begin to look backwards and reevalu-ate. After two seven-year cycles—because it's been fourteen years, right?—it was time for both of us to give it another try."

"So are we going to get blown out of the water?" I asked.

"I just don't know. I do know I'm nervous about it. I mean I have no idea how I'm going to do."

That night at the skippers' meeting, the race committee divided the fleet into four divisions. During the elimination series, there would be two starts, with the divisions being shifted around so that everyone had a chance to sail against each other. This meant that except for the people in your own division, you weren't sure who you were going to be sailing against, particularly when it came to the first race on Monday morning.

The start of Race One bore a disturbing resemblance to the beginning of the Midwinters: a chaotic blur of boats. Although I had a poor start, I caught a few good wind shifts midway up the first beat and then suddenly I saw Paul Fendler, just ahead of me. He might be two cell cycles away from the Paul I used to race against, but he still looked exactly the same in a Sunfish. He had a way of milking each puff for everything it was worth, leaning back as he rounded the boat slightly up and brought in the sail, that was a pleasure to watch—unless, of course, he was ahead of you. I could tell immediately that he hadn't lost a thing, at least when it came to sailing on shifty lakes.

Paul rounded in second, I rounded in third, but it wasn't until the second reach that I got close enough to hail him. Here we were, just where we'd left off fifteen years ago, nearly overlapped at the head of the fleet. "Hey, Paul," I said.

He did the classic double take. He had no idea that I was so close. "Jesus Christ, Nat, is that you?"

I nodded.

He laughed and said, "This is weird, isn't it?"

On the next upwind leg I found a few good shifts on the

right side of the course and passed Paul to lead at the mark. Two legs later, however, Paul found just the right winds to eke out a narrow win.

As I prepared for the next race, I knew that at least one thing hadn't changed after all these years: I still didn't like to lose, especially to Paul.

The Ultimate Captain's House

By the end of the elimination series, a general pattern had begun to emerge. Paul had burst out of the blocks with a masterful display of shift playing. Onshore, his wife and his mother operated as his support crew, even making sure he'd put on his sunscreen in the morning. Although his father wasn't at the regatta, he'd been the one who put together Paul's boat. From his home in Rye, New York, Paul had brought with him the same protective bubble of domesticity that had made my win at Barrington possible fifteen years before. I envied him, particularly at night in my motel room as I filled gouges in my daggerboard (its paint, applied more than fifteen years ago by my father, had begun to blister) and staved off waves of homesickness.

But at least I hadn't embarrassed myself on the race course. I'd been in the top five in almost every race. Unfortunately, it was a good news–bad news situation: I now knew that if I didn't finish in the top ten of the championship series, I'd be very disappointed.

And, of course, in the final analysis, how you finished in the qualification series had absolutely no bearing on what happened during the next three days. Jeff Linton had not even gone out on Tuesday afternoon, preferring to watch the racing from shore. As he sipped a drink and leaned back in his chair, he explained, "I wanted to see the racing from a different perspective—see if I could figure out these shifts." He peered across the lake, the Master of All He Surveyed. This was a guy who wasn't going to peak too early.

Bob Findlay, on the other hand, had been a bundle of nervous energy. When he wasn't dazzling the fleet with his boat handling on the race course, he was regaling the assembled multitude at the beer truck with jokes and stories. Bob had brought the dynamics of light-air Sunfish sailing to a new level, but whether he could maintain the necessary consistency remained to be seen.

If there was a solid sailor in the qualification series, it had been the Bahamian, Donnie Martinborough. No matter how unsettled the wind was, Donnie always maintained an inner calm. Others, too, had shown at least flashes of promise. What was going to happen come Wednesday morning was anyone's guess.

In the meantime, it was time I explored at least some of Springfield. This was, after all, the state capital and the home of Abraham Lincoln. That evening I was picked up at my Holiday Inn by three women in a huge green Cadillac with the vanity plate SUNFISH. At the wheel was Lee Parks, the person who came the closest to personifying the modern-day Sunfish class. Lee had worked for the Sunfish's manufacturer in the 1980s and now made a habit of attending just about every major Sunfish regatta. Her position at U.S. Sailing in Newport gave the class a vital and important connection to the sport's power base. Lee was accompanied by Texans Patricia Manning and Vicki Bremer. Vicki was the class's main correspondent, providing colorful, often hilarious accounts of regattas for the class newsletter, *Windward Leg*.

Spirits were high as we drove into Springfield, a city of wide streets and tall buildings that seemed almost deserted on this hot and humid weekday evening. On a tourist map we saw that several blocks just to the south of the city had been designated "Mr. Lincoln's Neighborhood," and after several jokes involving the children's show hosted by Fred Rogers (in whose real-life neighborhood I had grown up in Pittsburgh), we vowed to visit the area after dinner.

At an Italian restaurant deep within a warren of one-way avenues and streets, we rendezvoused with two more Sunfish stalwarts, Larry Cochran and Peter Beckwith, father of an old friend of mine, Alan Beckwith. It had been at Alan's wedding in September that I had first heard that the North Americans was to be held in Springfield, and I was particularly anxious to know how he and his wife Nancy were doing. Peter explained that the purchase of a new house and the impending birth of a baby had kept Alan (who'd won the North Americans in Springfield back in 1979) at home this year. It was a familiar story.

By the time we reached Mr. Lincoln's Neighborhood, darkness had settled over the city, and with the twinkling lights of a huge hotel looming behind us, we ventured into the nineteenth century. I couldn't help but compare this block of historic homes to downtown Nantucket, where mansions and stores built during the island's whaling era also kept the present at bay. While it was a community's heritage that was being sustained on Nantucket, these houses preserved the memory of a single man.

I realized that at least part of my comfort level on the comeback trail was directly proportional to my command of the history of the place I was sailing. Just as I had consumed Sarasota history before the Midwinters in March, in the week prior to the North Americans I'd read snatches of Carl Sandburg's biography of Lincoln. Now, as we wandered down an empty sidewalk, I remembered the words of Lincoln's Springfield law partner, Bill Herndon. For Herndon, Lincoln was a man of secrets and sometimes profound sadness, a man with truly extraordinary powers of concentration. But it was Herndon's description of the way Lincoln walked that spoke most powerfully to me:

> He put the whole foot flat down on the ground at once, not landing on the heel; he likewise lifted his foot all at once, not rising from the toe. . . . The whole man, body and mind, worked slowly, as if it needed oiling.

Approaching Lincoln's house, which still appeared just as it did in history books, I wouldn't have been surprised to discover its original owner's dark, scarecrow figure plodding down the road.

There was something in the quality of the Springfield

air—a dusty, voluptuous tang—that reminded me of Pittsburgh. This was how it felt to be inland. Out here in the middle of the continent, the land was the sea and the lakes were the islands; liquid islands that had served as my refuge when I was a teenager in Pittsburgh. Perhaps my move to Nantucket had been the culmination, rather than (as I'd always assumed) a repudiation, of my inland youth. I had been an islander all along. Lincoln had made a similar transition.

Even though he had grown up in the heartland, his destiny lay to the east, where he would steer our country through the stormiest seas a people can ever know. Here, a thousand miles from Nantucket, was the ultimate captain's house.

Day One

When I woke up the next morning, dread burned in my stomach and caused my fingers to quiver slightly; there was a dryness in my throat. Around 7:30 the phone rang. It was Melissa and the kids.

"Go get 'em, Daddy!" Jennie said. Ethan was also encouraging. "Break a stay, honey," Melissa said, and we both hung up. I stood in front of the bathroom mirror and painted myself with sunscreen, making sure to get the tips of my ears, which always burned. My daggerboard was in the bathtub where I'd been sanding it after returning from Mr. Lincoln's Neighborhood the night before.

On my way to the lake I stopped at a 7-Eleven and picked up a bottle of Gatorade and some bags of crackers. Driving down the little road to Lake Springfield, I found myself wishing the road might go on forever. I really didn't want to go through with this, did I? That morning it seemed as if I had everything to lose and little, if anything, to gain.

Things were very quiet as we rigged our boats. There were

sixty of us in the championship division. Unfortunately, there was absolutely no wind out on the lake. Aboard a pontoon boat, the members of the race committee surveyed the water's oily surface and shook their heads. There was nothing to do but postpone the start.

For the next four hours we waited onshore. At one point, Paul Odegaard, a past North American champion and light-air aficionado from Connecticut, put his boat in the water and went for a sail; at least it gave us all something to watch. Although the breeze was next to nonexistent, Paul demonstrated that there was at least something out there—tacking and jibing, even sailing backward at one point.

In the old days Paul Fendler and I would have been careful to hole up in opposite corners of the club, doing our best to keep our minds clear in preparation for the racing to come, but that morning we sat together and talked. Paul's wife and mother had gone off to do some sightseeing, and perhaps inevitably, we found ourselves discussing each other's personal lives, lives that we had been completely oblivious to back in the days when it had been only the racing that mattered. Now, even though we were on the verge of the finals of the North Americans, the personal stuff was what interested us.

Although we talked about many things, especially the decidedly nonnautical turns our lives had taken, it became clear that both of us, no matter how hard we'd tried to leave the past behind, had remained haunted by our years on the racing circuit. We both admitted to having dreamt regularly about sailing, even when it had been years since we'd raced a

Sunfish. My dream involved what I'd come to call the Never-Ending Sunfish Regatta, a vague sense of always sailing, always tacking on wind shifts, always tallying up the score, and always having another race to sail.

Paul's was more of a nightmare: A race is about to begin. Paul is there, ready to go, but discovers that he doesn't have his daggerboard. Searching frantically for it, he realizes that he also can't find his rudder, and where is his sail? As he runs around looking for the missing parts, the race starts without him.

Sometime after 1:00 p.m. a tentative breeze began to blow from the northeast, and the first race of the 1993 Sunfish North Americans finally got under way. I started toward the middle of the line and was in pretty good shape at the gun.

Since we were racing on a relatively small bay of Lake Springfield, the shoreline was never far away and had an inevitable influence on the wind. Indeed, much of what we were using to power our sails wasn't really wind at all; it was a thermally induced movement of otherwise stagnant air between the very hot land and the cooler water. As a result, it often paid to search out the thermals in the vicinity of the shore, an intensely green place of trees, lawns, and houses.

This meant that each windward leg posed a problem: Which shore do I go with? Choose correctly and you were golden; choose incorrectly and you were in the tank. But it wasn't simply a question of hitting the right side of the course; there were different ways to go about hitting it. There was the bold approach: Sail with reckless abandon to what is known as the corner of the course since it's there that you tack at roughly a 45-degree angle for the mark. Then there was the more conservative approach: tend toward what you think is the favored side of the course but tack on the little shifts you encounter along the way.

Since the last thing I wanted to do was begin this regatta the way I had started the Midwinters, I tried to have it both ways. I played the middle cautiously. Halfway to the mark, my indecision seemed to be paying off; I was in very good shape. Then in the last hundred yards thermally assisted boats began to pass me on either side of the course. I ultimately rounded in fifth, with Bob Findlay taking up where he had left off at the Midwinters in first and Donnie Martinborough and regatta organizer Todd Gay close behind. Now that we were in the finals, Todd had apparently put the distractions of running the event behind him.

The first reach was painfully slow and hot as the breeze gradually died to almost nothing. I rounded the jibe mark still in fifth, but during the second reach things began to happen. As the boats ahead sailed into lulls, I was able to stay in a patch of wind that moved me into second behind Martinborough at the leeward mark. Now we had what looked like an interminable beat ahead of us, with the wind barely twitching the strands of cassette tape I used for a wind indicator. With the wiggling strips of plastic leading the way, I began that second beat.

Donnie made a bold move to the left, the side that had paid off for him on the first beat, as did Findlay. I wasn't so sure and attempted to hedge my bet by remaining to their right. Meanwhile, behind us, a group of boats, led by Charlie Clifton's distinctive blue hull, hit the right corner hard.

Certainly I was doing well relative to Findlay and Martinborough, but in winning this particular battle, I was losing the war as a major shift and more wind came in on the right. The sensations that you experience at the moment when you realize that a race is falling apart before your eyes are difficult to describe. Findlay began to curse, tacking from port back onto starboard (away from what now seemed to be the favored side) with the angry bravado of a guy who wasn't about to give up the ship. Martinborough, ever the emotional Rock of Gibraltar, sailed on silently.

Meanwhile, I saw what seemed like a stationary band of air over on the left side of the course. I went for it and then did everything I could to stay in the wind line. I could feel my pulse rate climb as I worked a less than ideal situation for all it was worth, tacking back and forth with a quiet frenzy that soon had me drenched in sweat. Clifton's blue hull rounded first. Not far behind him were Todd Gay and Paul Fendler. After one last tack, I rounded in fifth.

The run down to the leeward mark was full of dangerous holes in the wind, but just behind me Dan Feldman, a big blond guy who liked to talk, kept things interesting. I've never been much of a talker on the race course; I can't concentrate on a race and speak at the same time. But this leg was so long and slow and Dan was so friendly that even I came out of my shell a little bit. As we beat toward the finish, Dan edged me out at the line to take fifth. Charlie Clifton hung on to win, with Paul in second and Todd in fourth. Donnie Martinborough scrambled to twelfth while Bob Findlay came in fourteenth. Jeff Linton had come in twenty-first, seriously jeopardizing his chances of winning the series.

It was too late to attempt another race, and as we sailed in I tried to say some consoling words to a fellow sufferer on the left side of the course. After an entire day in the broiling sun, he was in no mood to talk and flashed me a single-digit response.

I could take a hint.

Day Two

W<small>HAT HAD ME</small> worried at Springfield was the possibility of rain. In this heat, I knew my glasses would fog up and I would have a tough time seeing. Although I had managed just fine in rain during the River Race, those had been entirely different conditions: cooler, with fewer boats. With sixty boats on the line and relatively short courses, I needed all the vision I could manage.

Sure enough, Thursday morning brought with it a steady downpour. At least there was some wind—ten to twelve miles per hour—that allowed you to sit on the deck when sailing upwind. Unfortunately, it also had the effect of blowing the rain into my face, which only compounded the vision problem.

Instead of going out there and attacking the fleet, I began the day feeling intimidated by the conditions. What had been a lake of pure blues and greens was now a place of rain-whipped gray. The confidence I had been slowly building over the course of the last three days had suddenly vanished. It was the Midwinters all over again, and as I knew all too well, the problem wasn't really my eyes; it was inside my head.

The wind was directly onshore, and since we were already behind schedule the race committee got things going quickly, setting up a short triangular course with the starting line only about a hundred yards off the club docks. Before I knew it, we were in the midst of a starting sequence.

For me it was like watching a video (and a blurry video at that) on fast-forward—everything was happening in hyperspeed. The gun went off and so did the fleet as I plodded, Lincoln-like, up the first beat. The leg was so short that before I knew it I was rounding the weather mark, Sunfish swarming all around me like flies. Boats were everywhere, the rain was in my face, and none of it made sense.

By the time I reached the next-to-last leg—a run—I took the opportunity to watch the leaders beating up to the finish. Rod Koch, the defending champ, was in first, with Bob Findlay in second. They looked awfully confident and fast.

I finished in twentieth and wanted to scream. I was throwing it all away. Just because of a little rain. Up to windward, boats that had already finished were luffing, their skippers talking about the race and watching people finish. I thought I knew exactly what they were saying: "Wow, looks like Philbrick tanked."

In a matter of minutes we were starting the second race of the day. It did not go well. Once again I was back in the twenties and slogging my way around the course, reacting instead of taking charge. On the downwind leg, a sailor jibed behind me, rounded up, and hit my rudder with his bow.

Most people in this situation would probably have yelled at the guy and told him to do his penalty circles, which is, of course, exactly what he should have done. However, the guy gave me a plaintive, questioning look, as if to say, "I'm sorry; it was an accident. Do I have to do my circles?" Although I wasn't happy with the situation, I was not feeling particularly vindictive. I was doing lousy; he was doing lousy; what greater good would be served by insisting that he perform two penalty circles?

It didn't help matters when he passed me on the next weather leg, ultimately finishing a half dozen or so places ahead of my twenty-third. But I didn't care. I was in a colorless world of lapsed confidence and vanished hope. Cliques of top finishers killed time in the rain around me as I leaned back just to make sure my rudder was okay.

To my horror I discovered that part of my rudder had been broken, leaving it dangling like a broken wing. No wonder the steering had felt mushy. But I had been too distracted by my visual/mental problems to give my rudder the attention it deserved. If I had known then what I knew now that guy would sure as hell have done his circles!

Before I could start the next race I needed to make some major repairs. I sailed in to the club, tied up to the dock, took off my rudder, and went looking for help. Standing near the clubhouse snack bar was the Mother Teresa of the Sunfish class: Peg Beadle, then editor of the newsletter and the owner of a Sunfish equipment business.

The two of us ran to her van, where she rifled through

several bins of parts before finally pulling out a brand-new rudder cheek assembly. Once back at the Sunfish I took off the broken piece and tried to attach the new one in the driving rain. It was not easy. Besides a bolt, there were all these nylon pads and washers and nuts, and in the rain and with my less than ideal tools and with the fleet gathering only a hundred yards away for the start of the next race, the time pressure was intense. I was living Paul Fendler's worst nightmare.

At one point my hand slipped and I gashed my thumb on the sharp end of the spring that pops up the rudder. Soon my cockpit was full of blood as I struggled with the rudder. By now a group of half a dozen spectators had gathered to watch my frenzied repair in the rain. At last I got the rudder to the point that I could sail. But my thumb was bleeding terribly. Of course, Peg just happened to have a Kermit the Frog Band-Aid in her purse, and with the fleet assembled for the next race, I was off and sailing.

The starting sequence had already begun. I had no idea how much time was left. I was about two minutes away when the red shape went up on the committee boat signaling a start. Then, miraculously, another shape went up and two horns were sounded. It was a general recall. Too many boats had been over the line early to make it a fair start. I had been given a reprieve.

But it did not go well. Once again I finished in the twenties. At least I had been able to start.

At lunch I wasn't in much of a mood to talk. Three races had been sailed in as many hours; the regatta was now more than halfway through; and I had eliminated myself from contention. Although it would have been convenient to attribute all my problems to the damaged rudder, in the final analysis I knew that I had only myself to blame. While I'd been dithering about the rain, Jeff Linton, Bob Findlay, and Donnie Martinborough had moved into contention. And then of course there was my doppelgänger, Paul Fendler, whose performance had put him in the regatta lead.

On one level (the higher plane to which we all aspire), I was happy for him, but on another and more immediate level, I was full of self-loathing and envy. As we ate lunch and the rain tapered off, Paul was exceedingly gracious. He seemed genuinely concerned about me. Also at our table was Joel Furman, the class measurer, who before scoring a thirty-fifth had started off the day with two eighths.

In between bites of his sandwich, Paul said, "After the second race today, Joel told me I should move my gooseneck forward, so I gave it a try and I won the next race. It made a huge difference. I must have been pointing five degrees higher."

I perked up slightly. "Really?"

The gooseneck is a bronze ring that attaches the boom to the mast. By moving the gooseneck forward, the sail is shifted aft, and this can help you point to windward. I had thought my gooseneck was already about as far forward as it should go—seventeen inches from the forward tip of the boom.

"Where is your gooseneck, Joel?" I asked.

"Fourteen inches."

"Wow." Given the fact that this was a fairly delicate adjustment, a difference of three inches was major. Whether or not it was going to make any difference, Paul and Joel had at least given me something positive to do.

By the time the fourth race of the day got under way, I was in a completely different mind-set. For one thing, it was no longer raining. A film had been lifted from my eyes. For another, I liked the way the boat felt with the gooseneck in the new position. The helm felt light; I felt fast. But so did, apparently, the rest of the fleet. After three general recalls, the committee imposed the black flag rule, and not wanting to repeat what had happened at the Midwinters, I vowed to take it easy at the start.

With thirty seconds to go, I was at the windward end of the line, side to side with Don Bergman, a very fast master sailor. With ten seconds to go, Don started to sheet in the sail, and I went with him, but, fearful of being called over early, I held back slightly while Don crossed the line at full speed.

I got a very good start. Don, however, got a start for the ages—at the awards ceremony the next day, the chairman of the race committee would mention Don's start as one of the highlights of the regatta. Almost immediately he had a twenty-yard lead on the fleet.

Don, who had not had a particularly good series up until this point, was in no mood to fool around. Rather than worrying about covering the fleet, he tacked over to the right side of the course and ultimately rounded with a sizable lead. Without the courage of Don's convictions, I, too, stayed to the right, while someone over on the left did an amazing job of playing the shifts to round almost overlapped with me in second. It was Jeff Linton.

After two reaches and then a beat, Don was still in first, with me in second and Jeff in third. The breeze was dying and the three of us were well out ahead of the rest of the fleet. While Don and I sailed with a certain giddiness, Jeff sailed with a quiet confidence. During the long run down before the final beat, Jeff made a point of not mixing it up with me. He could have positioned his sail directly upwind of mine, but instead of pushing every situation for the maximum advantage, he had the big picture firmly in view. If he scored a third in this race, he was on track to win the regatta; if he did something stupid by playing around with me and had to do a penalty circle, he might blow it. So he hung in there and waited.

Given the fact that Jeff had begun the North Americans with a twenty-first, this unflappable mode of conducting business was all the more impressive. It was also just how it had been for me fifteen years before. I, too, had begun the finals of the North Americans with a bad race (an eighteenth, if I remembered correctly), made all the worse by the fact that in 1978 there were no throw-out races. But instead of getting rattled the way I had done this morning, I had taken it in stride, never finishing any subsequent race out of the top five. But if 1993 wasn't my year to be relentlessly consistent, I'd take erratically brilliant.

As we started the last beat to the finish, I knew exactly what I was going to do. There was a line of wind on the right side. Rather than tack on the shifts, I was going to keep my boat in that wind line and see what happened. Midway up the beat, I was in first. By the finish I was way out there, with Don in second and Jeff in third.

I had done it. With Paul and Joel's help, I had stopped my demons dead in their tracks. I had won a race and now, for the first time in the regatta, I couldn't wait for the next start.

Day Three

THE RACING INSTRUCTIONS required that six races must be sailed for there to be a throw-out. We had already sailed five going into Friday. But by two o'clock that afternoon, it was looking like we might not have a throw-out. Lake Springfield was a vacuum.

Although it was certainly in my best interest to sail a sixth race, there was one man who desperately wanted a race: Jeff Linton. Without it, Paul Fendler would win the regatta. However, if one more race was sailed, all Jeff had to do was finish within five boats of Paul and the regatta would be his.

Going out that morning, Paul seemed philosophical about the day that lay ahead. "Whatever will be, will be" had been a phrase both of us had bandied about throughout the regatta, and that morning it seemed to have a special relevance. Jeff Linton, I'd noticed, had been anything but philosophical. Even though there'd been virtually no wind, he'd been the first one on the water. Where the 95-degree heat had prompted most of us to load our cockpits with water bottles and fruit, Jeff, knowing that Paul weighed thirty pounds less than he did, had taken nothing more than a lifejacket.

Also in the hunt was Bob Findlay. If Paul and Jeff dragged themselves out of the top ten and Bob managed to win the race, he would win it all. Springfield's finest, Todd Gay, was also poised to take advantage of any disasters among the front-runners. For my part, I needed another gift from God to finish in the top ten.

The challenge for me was to maintain my intensity through the seemingly endless wait. But, finally, when the starting sequence began in the middle of the afternoon, I was ready. Jeff and Paul might have their mountains to climb, but so did I.

I was at the windward end of the starting line with twenty seconds to go when I realized that I was going to be over early. Rather than delay the inevitable, I sheeted in the sail, shot across the line and tacked around the committee boat as the starting gun went off. Luckily the black flag was not up, enabling me to restart without being disqualified. If this had happened to me the day before, I would have been devastated, but today it was a different story. I was not about to roll over and die.

Once across the line, I tacked onto port and headed toward the right side of the course. Although the wind was from an entirely different direction from the day before, I saw something familiar on the right side—a band of air, if not wind, that had some kind of motion to it. There were about a half dozen boats over on the right side of the course, with the rest of the fleet spread across the middle and left.

The wind was painfully light as I sat on the leeward side of the boat with my back bent underneath the boom.

Midway up the leg, I had begun to dig my way out of the hole I had made for myself at the start. By the end of the leg I was in the top ten, rounding in about seventh, just ahead of Jeff Linton and Bob Findlay. Paul was ahead of me, as was Todd Gay, but not by much. Meanwhile Malcolm Dickinson, skipper of the "sticker boat" in the River Race, had a huge lead.

If the beat had been a challenge, the two reaching legs became a true ordeal. The nearly nonexistent wind dropped. What few zephyrs there were came in from behind, inevitably bringing the fleet with them. Ahead I could hear Paul cursing as he attempted to jibe around the mark. Soon Jeff, Bob, and a legion of others had sailed past me. One of them was Charlie Clifton. As we rounded the jibe mark, he said to me, "Nat, do you realize you're going backwards?" It was true. I was going backwards beneath a searing sun. It was so hot that even my legs were dripping with sweat. I was so overheated and frustrated as I watched Paul, Jeff, Bob, and now Charlie go past me that I wanted to scream. Then someone did it for me.

We were about halfway down the second reach and headed for the leeward mark when the committee boat fired a gun. Thinking that the race was about to be canceled, the fleet began to cheer. But wait a second, instead of three shots, which would indicate cancellation, there were only two, meaning that the race wasn't being scrubbed, it was being shortened. Once we rounded the leeward mark, we had one more beat to the finish and only then, after a leg that might take hours in these conditions, would the 1993 North Americans be complete.

There was one competitor for whom the absence of the third gun was apparently the last straw. As soon as it became clear that the race must still go on, he leapt to his feet and began to scream: "I hate this stuff! It's driving me crazy! How are we supposed to sail when there's no wind?! I hate this! I hate this! I hate this!" At first I thought he was kidding, but as he continued to shout and jump up and down on the deck of his boat, it became clear that the sun, heat, and tension had taken their toll.

This wasn't the first time I'd watched someone start to crack under the strain of a regatta. I'd seen people break into fistfights on the starting line. I'd seen a competitor get so angry about being thrown out of a race by a protest committee that he'd let the air out of the chief judge's tires. I'd seen an otherwise well-adjusted Sunfish racer burst into tears when he accidentally fouled another boat. I don't care who you are; if the conditions are bad enough and the tension is high enough, any sailor has the potential to lose it.

Meanwhile, back on the hot, still waters of Lake Springfield, the guy finally ceased his ranting and collapsed onto the deck of his Sunfish. After a few seconds of stunned silence, people began to speak and then laugh, and then suddenly it was clear that the entire fleet had experienced a vicarious form of release through the outburst of a single competitor. I knew that I owed him a debt of gratitude. Despite the frustrations of the last two legs (I was now in about sixteenth), I was ready to give it one more try. But this time I wasn't racing against the fleet; I was racing the wind.

Once around the mark, I headed for the right side and that elusive breeze line. In the middle of the course Paul and Jeff were in the midst of a tacking duel, with Paul attempting to put as many boats as possible between them while slowly working his way to the front of the fleet. Jeff, however, was perfectly willing to suffer a little backwind if it kept him in touch with Paul.

Meanwhile, Bob Findlay was positioning himself for the mother of all comebacks, hitting the left side with a flamboyance that caught the attention of several younger sailors in the fleet who followed him into the left-most recesses of the course. If the breeze came in from that side, Bob just might pull it off.

Midway up the leg, I was off almost completely by myself on the opposite edge of the course. I was in some vague band of wind, but every time I tacked I would get headed and be forced to tack again. It seemed like I had worked myself into an alternative universe that had no connection at all to what the rest of the fleet was sailing in.

But if I kept getting headed, Bob Findlay, way over there on the left, began to look lifted on port tack. Then a breeze hit me. Suddenly I was ghosting along on starboard tack at what was, relatively speaking, a truly astonishing speed. Making it all the stranger was that there was no evidence of wind on the water.

Up ahead I could see that Malcolm, although not as far ahead as he'd been at the leeward mark, was about to finish the race with a well-deserved win. To leeward and ahead of me were Paul, Todd, and Jeff, all fighting it out for second. By this point the promise of the left side had begun to fade as the breeze I'd found on the right just kept on coming. Within fifty yards of the line, I passed Jeff and Todd. Up ahead was Paul, inching his way toward the finish. Wouldn't you know. No matter how much I might pretend that it was just me and the wind, in the end it all came down to my doppelgänger, Paul. Although I knew it would probably have no bearing on the final results, at that moment it meant everything in the world to me if I could pass Paul at the finish. He had passed me in the first race of the qualification series; let's see what happened now, eleven races later, on the last beat of the finals.

I sailed into a lull and quickly rocked my body to leeward to induce some heel, just the move I'd practiced during that cold rainy day at Pocomo Creek back in November. The boat rounded up as a small, infinitesimal puff of wind freshened the sail. The acceleration was just enough to carry me across the line in second place, a few feet ahead of Paul.

Jeff Linton ended up winning the regatta. Paul took second, and I, thanks to that last puff, wound up in seventh. Okay, I wasn't a champion again, but I had achieved a goal that I'd dared not hold myself to as recently as the day before: I'd finished in the top ten and close, oh so close, to the top five.

Jeff had seemed fated to win. Dick Tillman, a past Laser champion, said it best, describing a kind of road map to the Zone: "It's like you're on a trip of a thousand miles and you've already gone 999 miles before you even get to the regatta. You know all you have to do is go that last mile and the journey will be ended."

That night at the awards ceremony, after Jeff had received his ritual dunking in the lake, I surprised myself. I had expected to feel relief that at last it was all over. Instead I found myself asking people about next year's North Americans in Charleston, South Carolina, and then the Worlds in Bermuda. I was reluctant to see it end.

Maybe the Never-Ending Sunfish Regatta was more than just a fantasy. I sure hoped so. Because at that moment the future was looking pretty bright. I had just scored a first and a second, and I'd only just begun.

Epilogue

. . . But all these extravaganzas only show that Nantucket is no Illinois.

—Herman Melville, *Moby-Dick*

I RETURNED FROM SPRINGFIELD on a roll. I talked to Lee Parks at U.S. Sailing about bringing the Sunfish Worlds to Nantucket. Paul Fendler and I exchanged several phone calls, making plans for Paul and his wife Eileen to visit us on Nantucket that fall. By September my Nantucket history was at the printer.

But by October, I was beginning to feel a little lost. It had been almost exactly a year since I'd started my comeback, and already it seemed as if it had never happened. My Sunfish leaned against the house in exactly the same place it had been for all those years prior to my first sail on Gibbs Pond. Even the ivy was beginning to close in again.

At two o'clock on Wednesday, October 6, Melissa called from work.

"Want to go for a sail?" she asked.

At first I was caught so off guard that I didn't know what to say. All summer and fall Melissa had been extremely busy at work, with little time to do anything spontaneous or fun like sail or go to the beach.

Certainly the weather was perfect—a beautiful Indian summer afternoon with a twelve-knot westerly breeze. By that late stage in the season we had moved our Beetle Cat and its mooring out to Polpis, the small harbor near the heart of the island. We agreed to meet there at 3:00.

By 2:30 Jennie and Ethan were home from school. As soon as they'd had juice and a snack, they helped me load the canoe that served as our tender onto the car roof. With Molly in the back, we headed for Polpis. Twenty minutes later, we were paddling the canoe toward the Beetle. As Ethan and I pumped out the boat and Molly paced restlessly around the cockpit, Jennie paddled back to the landing to pick up Melissa.

The previous spring we had made the decision to buy, not just borrow, the Beetle Cat, and Ethan now went about the business of rigging the boat with a proprietary air. Although I'd been too busy with Sunfish racing and running the Nantucket Yacht Club's sailing program to spend much time sailing with the kids that summer, things were different between Ethan and me when it came to boats. We had the River Race behind us. Jennie, too, had changed. She could now row and paddle with confidence; she was also developing into a capable skipper.

Soon the boat was dry, the sail was up and luffing in the breeze, and Jennie had returned with her mother. After tying the canoe to the mooring, we were off, beating toward the western end of the harbor with the kids standing on the bow and clinging to the mast. Meanwhile, Melissa and I moved aft to help balance the boat, and as Molly lay on the cockpit floor with her head in Melissa's lap, we approached the center of the harbor.

I was soon lost in the sensations of a boat sailing upwind. The sun-warmed cockpit smelled of salt, sea grass, paint, varnish, wood, and rust. The bronze blocks on the boom squeaked with every adjustment of the sail; the tiller tugged at my hand with a fluttering nervousness as the hull's cedar planks flexed rhythmically through the wavelets.

The tide was high and still coming in, and Melissa suggested that we try sailing up nearby Pocomo Creek. I was stunned. Not only had she been the one to suggest that we go sailing in the first place, now she wanted to sail up a creek—just the kind of harebrained idea that had gotten me into so much trouble almost a year ago. I was all for it.

So we sailed from Polpis to Nantucket Harbor and hung a quick right into the creek entrance. With the wind and the current behind us, we were soon deep within a watery maze, jibing regularly as the channel wandered back and forth. Above us, two ospreys glided lazily in the clear blue sky, never straying far from their man-made platform and its ragged nest of sticks.

The farther we sailed, the narrower the channel became, and to prevent us from running aground Melissa stood up in the cockpit to help sight the channel. It occurred to me that unlike a year ago, when I'd hijacked the Beetle for that ill-advised journey through the mud, this time the two of us were working together as a team. It reminded me of our first summer together back in 1974, when Melissa would some-times crew for me in the 470, a hot rod of a boat in which the crew hung out over the water on a mast-suspended wire known as a trapeze. In waves, when the up-and-down motion of the boat threatened to knock her feet off the gunwale, Me-lissa would reach back and hold the forward corner of my lifejacket for support, a connection that inevitably sent a shiver of electricity down my spine. Now, almost twenty years later, there might not be thunderbolts, but I still felt sparks.

Eventually the creek's convolutions terminated at a wide tidal pool, a pond surrounded by a perimeter of marsh grass and a few houses. This was the destination I had been unable to reach in the rain last November. Now I was here in the yellow light of an October afternoon, and instead of being alone in a Sunfish, I was with my family in the Beetle.

With Jennie and Ethan once again up on the bow, this time to keep the rudder out of the mud, and Melissa playing the centerboard, I sheeted in the sail and began the long beat back. Soon we were tacking on an almost continual basis, the kids dancing around the deck like ballerinas as we swooped from bank to bank.

We'd emerged from the creek and begun to turn toward Polpis Harbor when I realized that Melissa and I were still sailors. Even after all these years, even after jobs and chil-dren, we still found joy in simply being together in a sail-boat. If there was one thing I'd learned in my comeback year, it was that there is no such thing as a singlehanded sailboat. Even in a Sunfish, I needed my family, my friends, and, yes, even my dog.

When it came to sailing, I had lost the Zone. Even when I was at my best in Springfield, I was too aware of my past, of having done it before. The Zone is not a place for looking back; it requires a fierceness, a single-minded commitment to the moment that I could no longer sustain. This didn't mean that I was all washed up. As I'd proven at the North Americans, I could still win a sailboat race.

But if I'd lost the illusion of mastery and control, at least I was no longer landlocked. I was sailing again on an island that was beginning to feel like home.

Now I understood. From a pond on Nantucket, to a bay in Florida, to a river in Connecticut, to a lake in Illinois, my comeback had always been leading me here—to a crowded sailboat on an island harbor twenty-four miles out to sea.

Acknowledgments

A WRITER INCURS A great many debts when working on a book, and thanks for this project are long overdue. First, I'd like to express my appreciation to everyone who has ever raced a Sunfish, especially Peg Beadle, Vicki Bremer, Charlie and Cindy Clifton, Paul Fendler, Joel Furman, Todd Gay, Jeff Linton, Patricia Manning, Lee Parks, and Alan Scharfe. Former Sunfish-class historians Rapid and Donna Buttner were a huge help. Thanks also to the friends, especially Marc Wortman, Mark Poor, Wes Tiffney, and Bruce Perry, who provided essential encouragement during my year of pond sailing.

Without the interest and insight of John Burnham, Doug Logan, and especially Peter Gow, this book would never have been written; without the enthusiastic support of Mimi Beman, it might never have been published. Thanks also to Mimi Harrington, Nancy Thayer, Tom Congdon, Paul Odegaard, and Stuart Krichevsky for their input regarding the ever-evolving manuscript. Island artists Illya Kagan and David Lazarus generously lent their support to the project. Wally Exman and Walter Curley at Parnassus Imprints were most helpful, as was Margaret Moore, curator at the Egan Maritime Institute. Special appreciation to Albert F. Egan, Jr., and Dorothy H. Egan, whose support through the Egan Maritime Institute kept me afloat during the writing of this book.

When it comes to the new Penguin edition of *Second Wind*, special thanks to my editor of nineteen years standing, Wendy Wolf, and to all the folks at Penguin, especially Kathryn Court, Patrick Nolan, and Louise Braverman. A special shout-out to my agent Stuart Krichevsky, who first read this manuscript back in 1998.

Finally, in addition to my wife, Melissa D. Philbrick, and our children, Jennie and Ethan, I'd like to thank the family that first put the wind in my sails—my parents, Thomas and Marianne Philbrick, and my brother Sam.